A Coastal Voyage in Watercolour

The Borders to the Humber

Ron Thornton

A Coastal Voyage in Watercolour
The Borders to the Humber

by Ron Thornton

First published October 2009
by Wagtail Press,
Steel, Hexham,
Northumberland
NE47 0HS
www.wagtailpress.co.uk

Book Design by T. W. Kristensen

Printed by Latitude Press

All paintings © Ron Thornton

ISBN: 978-0-9559395-0-1

The Journey Begins

The north east's exposed coastline and unpredictable seas have through the centuries presented local fishermen with very real dangers. It was essential that a boat was designed to cope with the often frightening conditions – hence the birth of the coble.

The distinctive design of the coble, with its flat horseshoe stern and narrow flaring hull has graced the north east coast for many centuries. From the Tweed down to Spurn Head, some 160 miles of coastline, these undecked fishing vessels have nestled in numerous harbours and even worked from open beaches such as Newbiggin by the Sea and Ravenscar. The basic design has Nordic influences – the Viking longboat with its high narrow bow to counter the rough North Sea, bears a striking resemblance.

The wooden cobles were developed and designed to suit local fishing conditions. Amazingly there were no plans or drawings. Each boat was built 'by eye' requiring great skill. No two were ever identical as each one was tailored to the needs of the new owner and the location from which they would be fishing.

The design of the coble has changed remarkably little over the centuries. In the 1930s the addition of an engine gave the coble greater independence from wind and tide. Prior to that they were rowed or used a sail.

Acknowledgements

My thanks go to my many friends for their help with this book, in particular Mick English for his scanning of my original paintings, Tom Kristensen for book design & layout, Peter Heath for additional graphic design, and Heather Redfearn for her secretarial expertise.

Also to those who assisted me with my research, including Ian Armstrong, Carl-Eric Carlsen, Graeme Cook, Margaret Cook, John Dawson (Secretary of The Six Townships Community History Group), Tony Edwards, Kathleen Gilbert, Margaret Gittins, Marshall Hall, Derek Hutchinson, Helen Janes, Hilary Kristensen, Steve Murphy, Vicky Pepys, Graham Ross, Neville Upton, Richard Walker. Thanks also to the staff of Hexham, Newcastle, Ponteland, Prudhoe and South Shields Libraries and to Liz Sobell for proof reading.

Also my friends at Stamfordham Art Club for their support.

I would like to thank Hilary Kristensen of Wagtail Press for her encouragement and guidance with this project. Thanks also to David and Jenny Thompson of the Forum Books and Art Shops in Corbridge who suggested that my first book "The River Tyne" and now this new book should be published.

A very special thank you to my long-suffering wife Ann for her patience and continued support, especially with typing and filing throughout this project. And to my daughter Wendy for her practical support and business acumen.

Should you wish to purchase signed original paintings or prints of the paintings in this book please email:

art@rwthornton.com

or visit our website: www.rwthornton.com

For Ann

St. Abbs

Contents

Introduction

The history of the Northumbrian Coast is a very troubled one. Throughout the Middle Ages this was regarded as the "Border Country" and was not an easy place to live. The Scottish and English armies fought bitter and bloody battles over many hundreds of years. Even when they took the odd break, local warlords and villains stepped in so there was little rest. Therefore it comes as no surprise that the northerly stretch of this beautiful coastline is bejewelled by spectacular castles and ruined fortifications that still stand proudly staring out to sea. This wealth of historical attractions, combined with miles and miles of empty golden sands and dramatic cliffs, produce what many consider to be one of the finest stretches of coastline in England.

To the south, beyond Wearmouth, with its cliffs and beautiful wooded ravines known as 'denes', lies the coast of Durham. This stretch of coast was at one time dreadfully contaminated by spoil from the many coalmines situated on the cliff tops. The last one closed as late as 1995. Unbelievably they simply dumped their waste onto the beaches and rocks below, turning them into stretches of foul sludge. Visitors kept well away. To visit them now, however, is a delight. The regeneration scheme, appropriately called "Turning the Tide", aimed to restore the beaches to their former glory and has been extremely successful. Fourteen miles of beautiful coastline are now available to the public once again.

Beyond Hartlepool sees the rise of North Yorkshire's splendid cliffs, in which many of the picturesque resorts huddle, on occasions precariously. Because of the many inlets and coves this part of the coast was a favourite for smuggling which was rife in the 17th and 18th centuries. The resorts here were initially built for the more affluent Victorians but with the advent of the railways, this stretch of beautiful coastline became available to the working classes and remain extremely popular to this day.

The Borders to Dunstanburgh

"The sea, the sea, the open sea
The blue, the fresh, the ever free
Without a mark, without a bound,
It runneth the earth's wide regions round.
It plays with the clouds, it mocks the sky,
Or like a cradled creature lies."

From "The Sea" by Bryan Waller Procter (1787-1874)

1. Cove Harbour
2. St. Abbs
3. Eyemouth
4. Burnmouth
5. Berwick-upon-Tweed
6. Holy Island
7. Budle Bay
8. Bamburgh
9. Seahouses
10. Beadnell
11. Low Newton-by-the-Sea
12. Dunstanburgh

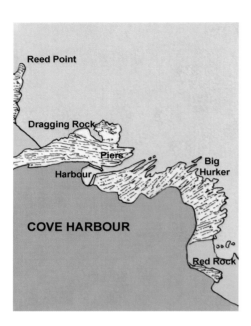

Reed Point

Dragging Rock

Piers

Harbour

Big Hurker

COVE HARBOUR

Red Rock

Cove Harbour

Cove Harbour is the seaport of Cocksburnpath. Rather a fancy title for a tiny basin which maintains one of the smallest fleets of full time fishing boats in all of Scotland.

Fishing at Cove goes back as far as the 1600s but was unable to expand significantly due to the lack of a proper harbour. During the 1750s Sir John Hall, the laird of nearby Dunglass, engaged a builder to construct a breakwater to provide some protection for moored vessels. The work was never completed due to the fury of a series of north east gales. When you consider the lack of technology at that time and the difficulties and dangers posed by the sea and winds, the mind boggles as to how and where they would even begin. What was achieved at the time was the cutting of a tunnel through the rock – no mean feat. Originally there were storage chambers in the tunnel but these have since been bricked up.

Further work, designed to help the fishing industry at Cove, continued over the years being regularly destroyed by raging seas. Finally in 1831 the present basin with its retaining sea walls was successfully completed. As well as fishing, sea transport was important for the distribution of a variety of general goods, minerals, timber etc. In the past this allowed for vessels of up to 60 tons to berth at Cove, weather conditions permitting. Part of the harbour is cut out of the living rock which also forms the basin, making it a rather dangerous place for small boats to lie. When the tide ebbs, the boats are liable to grind against the sharp rocks covering the harbour floor. The process is repeated when they begin to float as the incoming tide floods the harbour.

Cove can be difficult to find. Visitors must follow a rough path from Cockburnspath above Cove. There are only two inhabited houses which can be reached through the tunnel hewn through the cliffs - no wonder there are so few visitors. Having been there however, I fully recommend you make the visit. The scene overlooking the bay is quite breathtaking. The last time I visited there were only 2 vessels in the bay moored against the pier walls, whether they are still used for fishing is debatable.

Certainly in the past Cove has seen busier times where the fishing industry is concerned. A dreadful incident occurred at sea on the 13th October 1881 (it would have to be the 13th !) which became known as the 'East Coast Disaster', Due to extremely heavy and unexpected storms at sea 189 local fishermen were drowned, of these eleven men and four boats were lost from this tiny haven.

Cove harbour passed into public ownership when Dunglass Estates gifted the area to the old Berwickshire Council who passed it on to the Border Regional Council. In the late 1980s they closed the access road to Cove to vehicle traffic. This was done on the grounds of public safety due to the continued erosion of the cliff beneath the road. The closure effectively blocked the fishermen's access to their boat - fuel and fish would have to be transported by hand. Since then the road has been reopened for the fishermen to use.

R. W. Thornton

13

St. Abbs

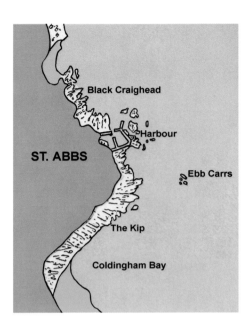

The headland used to bear the name of St. Aebbe, the daughter of the Northumbrian King Ethelfrith, who was shipwrecked off the Berwickshire coast (then the Northumbrian coast). She established a convent on the summit of Kirk Hill, located out on the headland. While Aebbe herself was noted for her own piety, the early years of new Christian establishment did not match her. She had difficulty enforcing discipline at the monastery. The monks and nuns were very lax and worldly wise. The nuns were reported to have bathed in the sea now occupied by St. Abbs harbour, using a wheeled device that allowed them to enter and leave unobserved (or perhaps not). St. Aebbe died in 679 AD and some two hundred years later the monastery was despoiled by Danish invaders. It is said that nuns, hoping to dampen Viking ardour, mutilated their faces.

The fishing port of St. Abbs was established in 1883, a mile south of St. Abbs Head in a rocky bay known as Coldingham Shore. Prior to any buildings the fishermen, who lived at nearby Fishers Brae, had to carry their fishing gear one and a half miles down a rugged path to reach the beach where their boats were moored. This path is now known as the Creel (lobster pot) Path. Quite a tiring experience before commencing a days fishing!

The first building in St. Abbs was constructed in the middle of the 18th century, followed later by a row of five cottages. Each had a central fireplace and a large chimney. The walls were built of "Chat and Clay", a framework of wood interlaced with straw and daubed over with moist clay. Today the lower village is overlooked from the cliffs by rows of what were originally fishermen's cottages, running parallel to the cliff edge. The upper part of the village is home to the church and a large stonebuilt mansion enjoying superb cliff top views.

St. Abbs became a very busy fishing harbour. Several of the larger boats owned by St. Abbs fishermen were based at Eyemouth – a mile to the south – on a permanent basis because of better berthing facilities. Those remaining in the harbour fish mainly inshore for crab and lobster caught by means of a creel.

In 1862 a lighthouse was built on the headland by David and Thompson Stevenson 225 ft. above sea level. Initially it was oilburning but changed to incandescent (carbide) light in 1906 and then finally to electric in 1966. A lifeboat station was first established in 1911 after the steamer, "Alfred Erlandsen of Copenhagen", bound for Grangemouth carrying a cargo of pit props, crunched headlong into the treacherous Ebbs Carr Rocks due to an unusually dense fog. The blaring of the ship's whistle brought the fisher folk rushing to the cliff head. Cries of help were heard through the thick fog, but there was little to be seen and therefore nothing could be done. St. Abbs then had no lifeboat, the nearest being at Eyemouth. A team of horses, pulling a four wheeled wagon containing rescue apparatus, negotiated the cliff tops to St. Abbs, a valiant effort but all in vain. Not a sound was to be heard from the wreck. However, while none of the crew made it ashore, there was one survivor. A dog, a powerful great dane, had managed to swim in the fog through the pounding waves and was found exhausted and terrified roaming the cliff tops. She was named Carra, after the rocks on which her master was killed. She became a local celebrity, going on to raise considerable sums of money for the Red Cross.

Scuba diving is a now a well established pastime. The clear waters off St. Abbs provide a dramatic contrast to the silt-laden waters to the north and south. These clear waters and spectacular under-water scenery resulted in Britain's first Voluntary Marine Reserve being established at St. Abbs in 1984. Shore diving to a depth of 50 ft. is possible from rocks outside the harbour wall.

R. W. THORNTON

Eyemouth

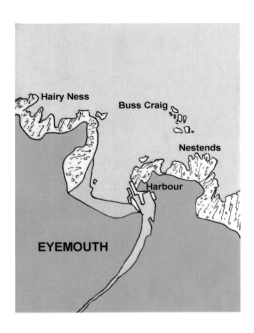

The town's name comes from its location at the mouth of the Eye Water. Eyemouth stands 8 miles north of Berwick-upon-Tweed. Its long history as a seaport can be traced back to William the Lion when the great Priory of Coldingham carried on a substantial maritime trade from Eyemouth. In 1214 a harbourmaster named Kinghorn was accused of overcharging a ship for anchorage dues. During the 16th century wars between Scotland and England, galleys landed French soldiers here for service with the Scottish armies. As a result the English established a fort on the northern cliffs overlooking the bay. Like many of its kind in these violent times it was demolished, rebuilt and once again destroyed.

Eyemouth Bay is protected by a ridge of rock to the north called the Hurkers. Many years ago there was a plan to unite them to the shore to form a complete breakwater. The idea was abandoned as the cost was deemed too high. In 1747 William Crow of Netherbyers planned the original pier and this was built by private subscription. The wide bay is flanked by high cliffs and has an attractive sandy beach. Despite being sheltered by the Hurker Rocks, storms generate immense waves that throw high plumes of spray over the sea wall named the Bantry. It is said to take its name from the Irish labourers who constructed it and lived in the fishing town of that same name in County Cork.

Fishing was first mentioned at Eyemouth in 1298. In 1897 it was not uncommon for boats to land off-line caught haddock. Eyemouth was also famed for its fleet of seine net boats. Seine netting became popular during the World Wars as it removed much of the backbreaking work endured by the fishermen's families. No one missed the bait collecting, line cleaning, baiting the hooks etc.

The 'Eyemouth Fishing Disaster' of 1881, previously mentioned, will never be forgotten. Twenty-three vessels from the Eyemouth fleet were lost; many swamped as they tried to battle their way back into harbour. That morning there was no warning of the impending storm. The day started out with bright, clear skies, calm water and not a breath of wind. During the afternoon one of the most violent storms ever experienced blew up within minutes. On land trees were uprooted and roofs were blown off houses. Boats, some up to fifty feet in length, were blown clean out of the inshore water where they were moored. That day Eyemouth lost 129 fishermen, many families lost all of their men-folk at a stroke. A tapestry, embroidered by local women, records the men and boats that were lost in the disaster and can be seen in the Eyemouth Museum.

Prior to the early 19th century, Eyemouth had the reputation of being a smugglers' haven, where large 'imports' of tobacco, spirits and tea were made. The old house, Gunsgreen, overlooking the inner harbour sited where the new Gunsgreen House now stands (see main painting) was reputed to have been built on the proceeds of smuggling. Local tales indicate that secret chambers and passages abounded for the storage of contraband and escape routes for smugglers. Some say that a concealed spring controlled a huge panel in the great fireplace in the kitchen.

Each year the "Herring Queen Festival" takes place. The Herring Queen and her Court are selected from pupils at Eyemouth High School. On a Saturday the Queen and her attendants, dressed in capes of silvered herring net, arrive by boat from St. Abbs, escorted by a fleet of flag-decked boats from the Eyemouth fleet.

R.W. THORNTON

Burnmouth

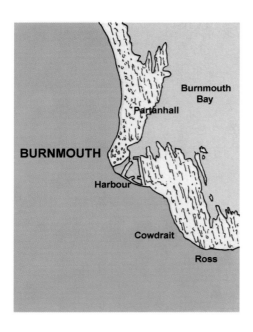

Burnmouth is split into two areas. Upper Burnmouth sited at the cliff tops adjacent to the A1 road, and Lower Burnmouth hidden away from sight at the bottom of the cliffs. Lower Burnmouth includes three further villages 'doon the brae'. Partenhall, Cowdrait and Ross make up the lower village. Partenhall is located towards the north, Lower Burnmouth sits by the harbour, Cowdrait is located towards the south harbour and the tiny community of Ross just south of Cowdrait. Ross now consists of only four houses and was considered a separate community as it lies just outside the parish boundary.

The village history is mainly that of a fishing community. Lower Burnmouth has been a working harbour since the mid 1800s. The fishing harbour was built in the 1830s. It was extended in 1879 and again in 1959. Sheltered from the north and north-east by outlying skeers and carrs, boats may enter Burnmouth Harbour when seas are breaking within the harbour walls of other ports. Today the boats fishing from Burnmouth concentrate mainly on crabs and lobsters. Larger vessels, owned by Burnmouth fishermen, now operate from nearby Eyemouth, although within recent memory seine net boats fished from Burnmouth. Regretably, Burnmouth did not escape the great storm of 1881, losing 24 men, which affected all the families living there.

Ross, the most southerly of the Lower Burnmouth communities, is surrounded by sandstone cliffs which have been sculpted over many years by the wind and waves into a series of attractive patterns and shapes. These formations are now designated as Sites of Special Scientific Interest.

Leaving Lower Burnmouth you ascend an extremely steep brae or bank to reach Upper Burnmouth at the top of the cliffs. Burnmouth has two pubs, the "Flemington Inn" and the "Gulls Nest" adjacent alongside the A1 main road. The Flemington had eye-catching pub signs on the north and south gables. For the traffic travelling south they come across, "The Last Inn Scotland", those travelling north, "The First Inn Scotland". Sadly the "Flemington" was gutted by fire in 2006.

In 1961 my wife and I spent our honeymoon in Burnmouth. Money was really scarce then and while looking through our local newspaper we saw bed and breakfast advertised for £5 per week at a place called Burnmouth of which we had never heard. A relative kindly drove us from South Shields up to the Coast to Burnmouth and halfway down the steep brae to a house which overlooked the harbour below - a heart-stopping vista. We loved it so much that we returned for the next eight years, latterly accompanied by our daughter.

I went fishing with the local fishermen and enjoyed a few pints with them in the Flemington. It took a while to overcome the language, but when I did the local gossip was worth waiting for. One trick I did learn and still use to this day, was watching the fishermen drink a half of beer, never a pint, along with a nip of whisky. When they finished the whisky they would pour a mouthful of beer into the whisky glass, swill it around and then gulp it down so that they wasted none of the whisky – Canny Scots !

R.W. THORNTON

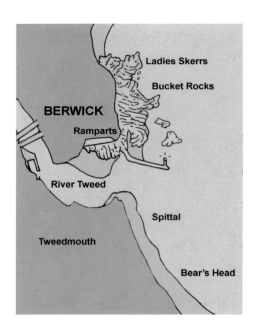

Ladies Skerrs
Bucket Rocks
BERWICK
Ramparts
River Tweed
Spittal
Tweedmouth
Bear's Head

Berwick - upon - Tweed

Berwick lies almost equidistant from the rivers Forth and Tyne. It stands on a steep hill on the northern bank of the Tweed where the wide estuary narrows. On the opposite side of the river lies Tweedmouth which provides a deep water anchorage. Berwick is a lively place with interesting narrow streets, Dutch-tiled roofs and many notable architectural features. These include the barrack buildings and striking defence ramparts with wonderful views along the coast.

In the early days Berwick was the most prosperous port in Scotland, largely due to its strategic position on the English–Scottish border. Unfortunately this led to a succession of raids, sieges and changes of ownership resulting in Berwick experiencing a more violent past than any other town in the kingdom. Between 1147 and 1482 the town changed hands between England and Scotland no less than 14 times. One of the most brutal raids was by King Edward of England (known as Longshanks – he was well over 6 feet tall) in 1296. He butchered the inhabitants and those who were not burned to death were put to the sword. It was said that the blood of some 8,000 men, women and children washed down the streets and into the Tweed which was coloured a deep red as it flowed out to the harbour.

Over the years the harbour has been significantly improved. A new pier was built on the Berwick side, Berwick Quay was extended and a stone jetty was constructed on the Tweedmouth side at Carr Rock. The foundation stone of the pier was laid in 1810 and completed in 1825. Admiral Stow laid the foundation for a lighthouse at the end of the pier in 1826 and the structure was completed within the year.

Throughout the years Berwick has continued to prosper, enjoying such economic activities as fishing, shipbuilding, engineering, sawmilling, fertiliser, stone and grain production. Berwick's herring fleet declined but salmon fishing still remains important to this day, and the Tweed is still regarded as the most prolific salmon river in the country. The exporting of salmon takes on a whole new twist when one learns that in the 1730s an enterprising Berwick man transported salmon by road, using six horses, to London. He is reputed to have made a profit of £20 on the round trip, quite a sum in those days.

Eventually it was discovered that on the Continent it was customary to pack salmon in ice to keep it fresh on long journeys. This technique was introduced in Berwick in 1788 with great success. Ice houses were built on Carr Rock for the storage of ice, some 7,600 cart loads of ice were collected each winter – not the most pleasant of jobs. The ice was used to preserve salmon in the smacks, small boats which then raced south under canvas to the Thames.

The old Berwick Bridge is the fifth to have been built on the same site. The first bridge here was a rickety wooden affair. The tale is told that the then king, James VI, was so frightened by its shaking when he crossed it, that he threw himself off his horse and fell into the river. As a result he demanded that a safer bridge be built. The Old Berwick Bridge is a stone-arched bridge with 15 spans and is some 1200 feet long. It was started in 1609 and was not fully completed until 1634. Later two further bridges were added. The Royal Border Bridge was designed by Robert Stephenson in 1846 and came into use three years later. The most recent bridge was erected between 1925 and 1928 and was designed and built by L.G. Monchel & Partners, establishing at the time two records: it was the longest road bridge in Britain (1410 feet) and contained the largest reinforced concrete arch, with a colossal span of 361 feet.

R.W. THORNTON

Holy Island

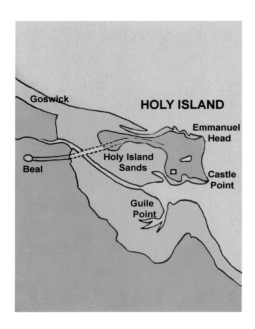

Lindisfarne, or Holy Island, is a tidal island that lies on the north east coast just below Berwick. A causeway built in 1954, roughly three miles long, connects the island to the mainland and floods twice a day by tides – restricting access to and from the island. The original old route across the sand, known as the "Pilgrims Way" or "St. Cuthbert's Way", can still be walked, tides permitting, the crossing being marked by wooden posts. Sir Walter Scott summed up the situation in the following poem.

> "Dry shood o'er sands, twice every day,
> The Pilgrims to the Shrine find way;
> Twice every day the Waves efface
> Of staves and sandelled feet the Trace".

The name Lindisfarne comes from Lindis, a small tidal river and Farne, meaning "retreat", and first appeared in the history books in 634AD. When Oswald became King of Northumbria he invited St. Aidan to Lindisfarne to help the natives of the area to renounce their pagan customs – they appeared to be a 'rough lot'. The well chronicled St. Cuthbert, a former shepherd boy from north of the Tweed, succeeded St. Aidan in 664AD. In 676AD he retired to a 'cell' on the nearby Farne Islands where he died in 687AD, worn out by the rigours of his self-imposed exile. The monks brought his body back to Lindisfarne. Eleven years later they had cause to dig up his body and to their amazement found it undecayed. They redressed it in new robes and replaced it in an open coffin. After a series of Viking raids the Monks fled the island and found their way to Durham where St. Cuthbert now rests.

In 700AD soon after St. Cuthbert's death the Lindisfarne Gospels were created, written on parchment made from the skins of some 100 calves and beautifully illustrated by Eadfrith, who later himself became Bishop of Lindisfarne. It now resides in the British Museum – much to the annoyance of many northerners.

Lindisfarne has been known for its fishing from as early as 1372. The monks possessed an oyster dredger for gathering shellfish from the Fenham Flats in the late 1300s. The island was once a haven for the great herring fleets that fished the east coast of England and Scotland. Indeed during the reign of Queen Elizabeth I there were merchantmen and the Queen's ships moored here. During these times the islanders were considered lawless, being involved in smuggling and wreck plundering. Such lawlessness was not helped by the fact that there were at one time over seven pubs on the island. Doors opened at 6.a.m. when the fishermen called for their drams of whisky (3d a half) or rum (4d a noggin) before setting off for a days fishing. Sadly today there are few signs left of the fishing. Small boats still fish but mainly for crab and lobster. Several of the larger fishing boats were upturned on land, sawn in half, had windows and doors inserted and now act as sheds to store equipment.

The castle was built in the mid 16th century under the direction of King Edward V1 as fortification against the Scots and to protect the harbour. It was bought by Henry Hudson who established the 'Country Life' magazine in 1902, and was converted into a private house by the famous architect Sir Edward Lutyens. The castle is now in the hands of the National Trust.

The limekilns, adjacent to the castle, are worth a visit. Lindisfarne has a long lime-burning history and the kilns are among the most complex in Northumberland. A horse-drawn wagonway linked the kilns with the limestone quarries on the north and two new jetties were built west of the castle. Fragments of these jetties can still be seen. Apparently the island used to teem with rabbits giving rise to another commercial enterprise. Crabs with lighted candles attached were sent down the burrows and the rabbits were netted as they tried to escape.

R.W. THORNTON

23

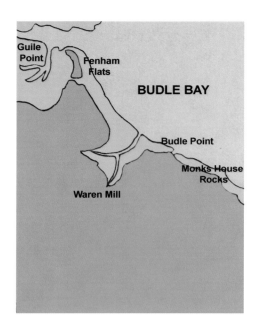

Budle Bay

In the 13th century, when Berwick was still part of Scotland, Warenmouth on the southern shore of Budle Bay was the most northerly port in England and was given its charter by King Henry III. Later known as Newtown, the importance of this once bustling grain port declined as Berwick passed permanently into English hands. In 1482 the harbour fell into disuse.

There is a small haven in Budle Bay, about a mile and a half south of Holy Island called Waren Mill. It used to be the port of both Bamburgh and Belford. The latter was a small market town where large quantities of corn were sold for export. Waren Mill was typical of the undeveloped tidal havens used by small coasters during the Industrial Revolution. Too shallow and inconvenient for sailing vessels, Waren Mill was the anchorage for locally owned boats of some 50-100 tonnes. One of them, "The Dapper", was an 80 tonne brig built at North Shields in 1814. She traded regularly between Waren Mill, Newcastle and Berwick before her loss in 1847.

The 18th century mill on the roadside at the head of the bay occupies a site where mills have stood since 1187, the first mill being a water-powered corn mill. Ships that arrived with corn to feed the mills and then carry away cargoes of flour revived the harbour's fortunes during the 19th century. The industry declined and the last grain ship to enter the port was in December 1881. The old quay, the remains of which still stand on the south shore of Budle Bay, was rebuilt around 1912 to handle cargoes of whinstone from nearby Kittling Hill quarry. This trade ended only a few years later. The corn mill and old warehouses overlooking the bay have been converted into luxury apartments, affording wonderful views of the bay and sea.

Today the only arrival and departures into the bay are a splendid range of waterfowl such as brent, greyling geese, redshank, wigeon, ringed and grey plover. They find sanctuary and a plentiful supply of food in this beautiful bay which is a popular haunt for birdwatchers.

R.W. Thornton

Bamburgh

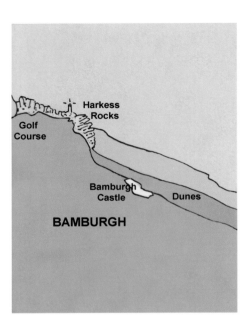

Bamburgh is a very ancient site. There are signs of Roman occupation and possible earlier tribes who recognised the military advantage of a 150 ft rock covering some 8 acres, perched above the sea and surrounding flat land. The castle was occupied in 547AD by the first Northumbrian King who was called Ida the Flame Bearer. A later King of Northumberland, Ethelfrith (598 – 616AD) married Queen Bebba and as a wedding present he renamed the castle Bebbanburgh (Bebba's town). The high point of the castle's development occurred during the reign of Henry III.

It is interesting to note that the castle was very badly damaged during the Wars of the Roses by the newly invented cannon fire, making it the first English castle to be attacked by artillery. Because of the ongoing sieges over the centuries, Bamburgh languished in ruins until 1704 when its fortunes were restored. It was bought by the Bishop of Durham, Lord Crewe. He made many positive changes, some aimed at supporting the local residents, including opening a boarding school for local girls to train as domestic servants. There was a free surgery and dispensary. A windmill and granary were also established. Horsemen roamed the immediate shores after gales looking for shipwrecked sailors who were then accommodated in the castle. Lord Armstrong of Cragside Estate purchased the castle in 1894 and carried out major restoration work.

Despite the popularity of the castle Bamburgh village remains unspoilt. A village green, tearooms, inns and attractive cottages make it worth a visit. I have played cricket a number of times on the ground immediately below the shore side of the castle and have never played against such a dramatic backdrop. The village church is over 800 years old and has a poignant reminder of times past, with a low window where plague stricken villagers could receive communion without entering the church.

We cannot leave Bamburgh without a mention of an international heroine, Grace Darling. Grace was born in the village in 1815, the daughter of William Darling who became keeper of the Longstone Lighthouse on the Farne Islands. She was 10 years old when the family moved to the island. On the seventh of September, 1838, a luxury liner, the "S.S.Forfarshire", struck rocks during a raging storm. Grace, who had spotted the wreck first, accompanied by her father, braved the appalling elements and rowed out to the wreck. Their coble measured just 20 ft. in length and only 6 ft. wide. They managed to save eight men and one woman, but forty three passengers drowned. Having survived the dangers of that dreadful night, Grace, a pale and shy 22 year old died of consumption four years later. During these four years her heroism became legendary and was celebrated throughout the land. Offers of marriage and money flooded in. She was even offered the vast sum then of £10 per week to row her coble across the stage at the Adelphi Theatre in London twice a night. The Grace Darling Museum first opened in Bamburgh in 1938 and has recently been redeveloped and updated.

R.W.Thornton

Seahouses

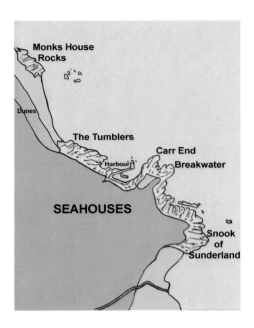

Seahouses has become one of the most popular tourist centres on the Northumberland coast, well known for its ice cream parlours, amusement arcades and mouth-watering fish and chips. It is the main departure point for the Farne Islands, an extremely popular boat trip in the summer. If you do make a boat trip across to the Farnes, some 2 to 5 miles, make sure your fish and chips are eaten well beforehand in case of choppy seas – not a good combination! However the working aspect of Seahouses is still visible when you visit the harbour. There are still fishing boats to be seen with their backdrop of colourful creels (lobster pots), fishing nets and marker buoys.

 Northsunderland/Seahouses, to give the village its full name, is well known as a fishing village. Alas, very little is left of that illustrious heritage of the 1800s. Initially the harbour was used for the shipment of large quantities of corn and in the summer of 1846 over a thousand tons of corn were shipped out. During the 1770s the quarrying and burning of limestone arrived - hence the limekilns which add character to the harbour. The quicklime was shipped to Scotland, mainly for fertilisers. An early comment by a visitor in 1858 indicated that 'Lime is the principle article of trade; and the kilns are built close to the harbour for convenience of loading and for the inconvenience of the town which gets well-smothered in smoke whenever the wind blow from the sea.' Apparently doors and windows were shut and very few people ventured outdoors.

The lime trade ceased in 1860, making the town cleaner but very much poorer. Fortunately industry had been steadily expanding from the 1840s. Some 52 herring boats were based in the harbour by 1855. The herring boom of the 1860s brought a great deal of work to the harbour and a large influx of the 'fisher women' who followed the fleet down the coast to prepare, cure and pack the fish. They worked extremely hard in dreadful conditions but on a good day could make as much as ten shillings, quite a tidy sum in those days. At that time there were up to ten separate fish curing centres in the town.

The harbour piers were in poor condition, the entrance channel between them being only 18 metres wide. They embraced an acre of water that completely disappeared at low tide. Improvements were discussed, plans were shelved and no decisions made - nothing changes! Eventually the size of fishing boats wishing to use the harbour was dramatically increased. There was a significant reduction in the number of vessels using the harbour but a large increase in overall capacity spurred those in charge into action. Work commenced in 1886 and the new harbour was completed by June 1889. However, the outer harbour was still tidal and could only be used by smaller, lighter draught vessels which could be laid up on the harbour bed. Eight large herring boats were permanently based at Seahouses within the inner harbour by 1905. These were supplemented by up to 140 boats from further along the coast during the herring season. The boats were laid side by side right across the inner harbour, a sight worth seeing.

In 1974 significant improvement work was carried out. The harbour was deepened to provide faster turn around times for the remaining fishing boats. A new launching slip was built to partly benefit the long established boat building yard of R. Dawson and Sons. They constructed traditional wooden built vessels and were the only such yard in Northumberland. Sadly Dawsons' closed in the 1990s. Today there are arguably more pleasure craft and boats ferrying visitors out to the Farne Islands than there are active fishing boats sailing from this attractive harbour.

R.W. THORNTON

Beadnell

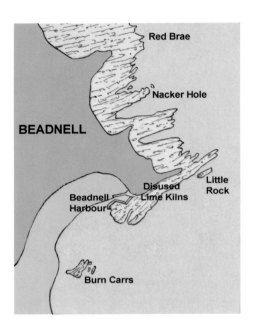

Beadnell is a very attractive little harbour, the only west facing harbour along the whole of the north east coast. Its clean sandy bay and sheltered waters have attracted windsurfers and sailing yachts over the years. Above the harbour are the well known lime kilns which remind one of the ruins of a castle, with their high, rounded arches leading into gloomy passages where today's fishermen store their nets and lobster pots. The harbour was built in 1798 by local landowner John Wood. He signed an agreement shortly after with Richard Pringle to build the lime kilns, lime being widely used in agriculture at that time. The Woods were evidently astute business men, leasing out brick-clay workings, coalmines on the south links, saltpans on the shore, and the limestone and freestone quarries which gave Delf Point its name. Windmills powered the workings and later, a horse drawn railway carried the limestone to the kilns. They also reorganised Beadnell's fishing industry. Until then the catches were crab and lobster.

It was Wood who introduced the very profitable herring fishing and curing system which eventually became Beadnell's most important industry and the harbour kilns fell into disuse.

Travel back a hundred years or so and the village consisted of just 49 houses, yet in summer up to ten 50ft. keel boats and 60 local fishermen operated from the harbour together with boats from Scotland, Ireland and Cornwall. The distance the latter two had to sail to even reach the fishing grounds is remarkable. Beadnell women helped by the Scottish fisher lasses worked long hours in the village's three yards packing fish into barrels. There was no rest for them in winter. The time was spent baiting hundreds of hooks with limpets and mussels - and gossiping. I'll bet there were few secrets in the village! The men spent their winter days fishing for haddock and cod from smaller sailing cobles.
Regrettably all this was about to change. Beadnell's herring fishing declined with the introduction of steam drifters and the approach of World War I. However around the same time the holiday industry began to develop.

In 1947, Sir John Craster donated the harbour to the remaining 25 Beadnell fishermen and their successors still own it today. They continue to fish for crabs and lobsters, joined now by boats from other villages.

Interesting links with the fishing past are the wrecks of two boats which, depending on the tides, can be seen offshore, the Mistley" and the "Yewglen".

Beadnell certainly has an interesting past. When a wooden hut was being built in 1934 close to the harbour, two Bronze Age sandstone cists were unearthed. They contained crouched skeletons of a man and a woman, with the remains of a pottery food vessel. On the grassy banks nearby at the entrance to the harbour, the ruins of a 13th century chapel were dug from the wind-drifted sands a hundred years ago. The walls, some 5ft. in height, were unusual in that they were cemented in clay rather than lime which would seem to reduce any permanency. Regrettably most of this unusual find was damaged by soldiers digging trenches for the First World War.

The name Beadnell comes from more than one source. Once pronounced by local residents as 'Beadlien' it is thought to derive from either the name 'Bedewine' or from 'Bede's Hal'. A pele tower was built to provide refuge during the times of the Border troubles.

R.W. THORNTON

31

Low Newton-by-the-Sea

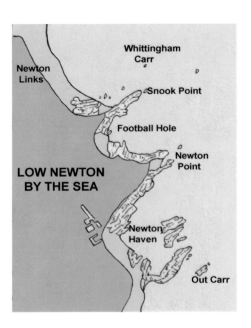

Low Newton by the Sea, also called Newton Seahouses, was built in the early 19th century to house local fishermen. It is considered by many to be one of the most picturesque villages along the north east coast. The village is an open-ended square of whitewashed cottages surrounding a very attractive village green. There are wonderful views looking out over harbour and sea at Newton Haven. The population then was said to be about 250, a lot of people for such a tiny settlement. Today with the fishing gone, the sheltered bay provides safe anchorage for small craft and larger yachts. It has also played a part in the development of windsurfing.

Within the Square nestles the hugely popular "Ship Inn", originally called "The Smack Inn". It would be difficult to imagine a more local 'local'. Under new management, a microbrewery has recently been installed with real ale brewed on the premises. Some of the names are worth recording - *Sea Wheat*, *Sand Castles at Dawn* and *Ship Hot Ale*.

Low Newton by the Sea is approached from High Newton by the Sea, roughly ¾ mile inland. High Newton by the Sea is something of a puzzle. It certainly may be high but definitely not by the sea! The road from there runs down the hill towards Low Newton. On the road just above and part of the village, stands a group of buildings. Here lies St. Mary's Church, dating from the 19th century which is a most unusual building. The Church was bought in 'kit' form and is constructed from corrugated metal sheeting and attractive stained glass windows – an unusual combination! The building was extensively refurbished a few years ago and continues to serve as a church and village hall, playing an important part in community life.

Three pill boxes dating from World War II still guard the beach at Newton Links. The area is well known for its bird watching facilities. The 'Newton Pool Bird Reserve', overlooking Newton Pool is worth visiting.

I have first hand knowledge of the "Ship Inn". When I lived in Craster I became a member of the lifeboat team. We used to go out for practice runs in the inflatable vessel – usually three of us. One of these 'runs' entailed heading north up the coast. To my surprise we beached the vessel at Low Newton, dragged the boat up beyond the watermark and enjoyed a pint in "The Ship".

Many years later we moved to Riding Mill near Hexham, some 95 miles round trip from Newton by the Sea. To my delight I got to know someone in the village who had a boat moored at Low Newton and was looking to make up a four man crew to go line fishing. Leaving the village at 6.00 on a Saturday morning we travelled to Newton, where we put out to sea from the harbour and fish the coast for about 4 hours. In those days fish were plentiful and we used to return to Riding Mill and give them away to friends and neighbours – I was very popular! It goes without saying that we popped into "The Ship" before coming back home. I considered myself a regular.

On another fishing trip, we had a kitty of a pound a head for the first to catch a fish. After a bad run I decided to take matters into my own hands. I kept a small cod from the previous trip and put it into the deep freeze. I smuggled it back on the next visit, tied it to my line without anyone seeing me and dropped it into the sea. Within 2 minutes I hauled it aboard, shaking the line so that it "wriggled" and collected the kitty. When we were in "The Ship" I confessed my wrongdoings and returned my ill-gotten gains.

R.W. THORNTON

Dunstanburgh

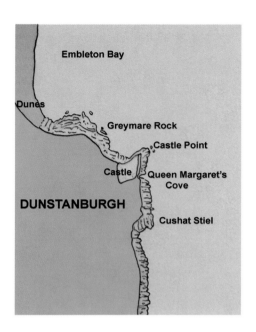

Embleton Bay
Dunes
Greymare Rock
Castle Point
Castle
Queen Margaret's Cove
DUNSTANBURGH
Cushat Stiel

Dunstanburgh is the largest of the Northumbrian Castles with a coverage of eleven acres, standing on magnificent basalt cliffs overlooking the sea just north of Craster. In 1313, Earl Thomas of Lancaster began construction of the massive fortress and the first quarry was opened up on May 7th 1313, probably at Newton, two miles to the north. By the time of his execution in 1322 the castle was virtually complete. John of Gaunt improved and strengthened the castle in the late 14th century.

During the Wars of the Roses the castle was a formidable stronghold of the Red Rose based in Northumberland and saw plenty of action as it changed hands at least five times. Each time it was besieged by cannon fire, and when the wars finally ceased little was left of the castle. In 1550 it was reported by Sir Robert Bowes that it was, "in wonderful great decaye".

It was never repaired and suffered even more by the removal of its stones, etc., being used for further building. The main building is to the south and consists of the entrance gateway and two semi-circular towers which would have risen to some eighty feet when first built. On the landward side the castle is defended by an unfinished dry moat cut into the rock.

The grand plan covers some eleven acres. There is no wall on the north side of the castle as the dramatic vertical drop into the sea makes a defensive wall unnecessary. However, the southern approach required guarding. Consequently a keep was built over eighty feet high containing the living quarters. The Margaret Tower to the east, with marvellous views over the sea and rocks was thought to be the site of the latrines. The tower apparently was named after Queen Margaret when she stayed there. The creek below is known as Queen Margaret's Cove. The harbour, though small and difficult to access, was used to anchor Henry VIII's fleet in 1514. Pieces of spar found at the foot of the cliffs are known as 'Dunstanburgh Diamonds'.

We cannot leave the castle without mentioning the famous Rumble Churn. Centuries of incessant pounding by the seas has produced crevices and winding channels far inland under the cliffs eighty feet below. As the waves surge into this cabin they carry with them pebbles and rocks that produce an extremely loud rattling, roaring noise – hence Rumble Churn. It is said that here the ghosts of drowned sailors wail before a storm.

"Loud was the roar on that sounding shore;
Yet still could the knight discern,
Louder than all, the swell and the fall
Of the bellowing Rumble Churn.

The spray as it broke appeared like smoke
From a sea volcano pouring;
And still it did grumble and rumble and tumble,
Rioting! Raging! Roaring!"

Apparently Dunstanburgh Castle has more than its share of ghosts. It is said that the ghost of Thomas Earl of Lancaster still walks the grounds. He died an extremely violent death for treason in 1322. It took the executioner no less than 11 strokes to decapitate poor Thomas. The ghost of Margaret of Anjou has also been seen wandering the castle grounds. A young knight known as Sir Guy the Seeker is also seen in ghostly form within the ruins.

R.W. THORNTON

Craster to the Tyne

"I'm on the sea! I'm on the sea!
I am where I would ever be;
With the blue above, ad the sea below,
And silence prevails whereso'er I go.
If a storm should come and awake the deep,
What matter; I shall ride and sleep."

from "The Sea" by Bryan Waller Procter (1787 - 1874)

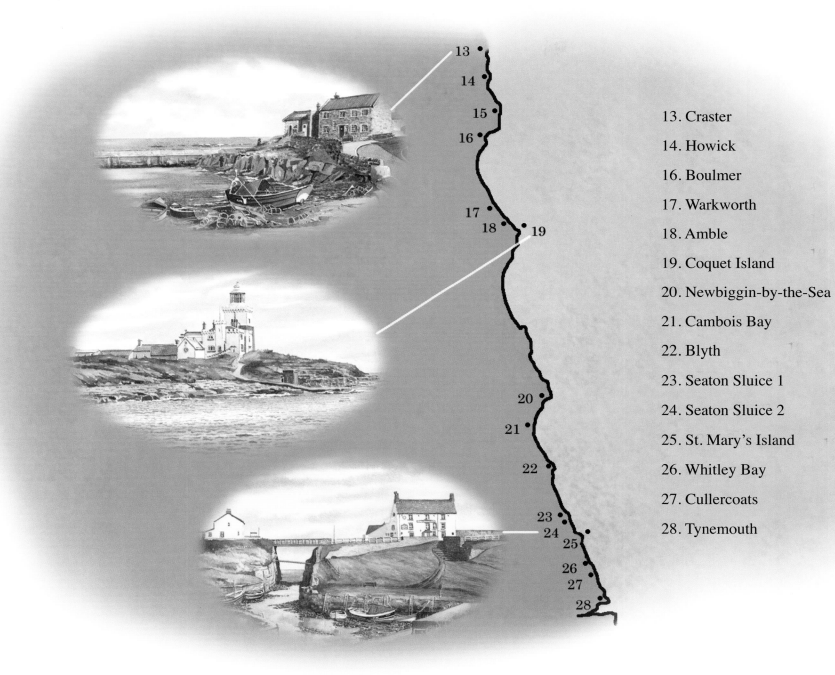

13. Craster

14. Howick

16. Boulmer

17. Warkworth

18. Amble

19. Coquet Island

20. Newbiggin-by-the-Sea

21. Cambois Bay

22. Blyth

23. Seaton Sluice 1

24. Seaton Sluice 2

25. St. Mary's Island

26. Whitley Bay

27. Cullercoats

28. Tynemouth

Craster

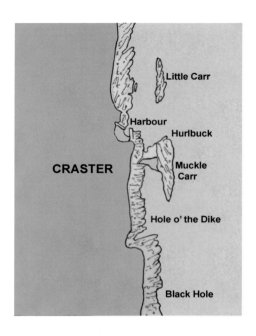

The village of Craster owes its name to the Roman fort of Crawchester that stood above the present site and has served as a natural harbour for fishermen over the centuries. In 1626 there were 8 residential fishermen. An indentation in the whinstone beds provided Craster with a natural harbour further protected by areas of rock known as Muckle Carr (Big Carr) and Little Carr.

Albert Craster was the founder of the Craster family, one of the biggest in Northumberland. They built Craster Tower, an imposing building, a mile inland from the Coast. At this time and until the late 18th century, Craster Village was still at the top of the hill, immediately north and east of Craster Tower. A map of 1723 indicates 12 houses in 2 rows. The present road did not exist and there was nothing between the houses and the sea apart from the little cove where the fishing boats were beached. By 1822 the relocation of the village and the development of the harbour was complete.

The present harbour was built by the Crasters in 1906, in memory of Captain John, killed during active service in Tibet in 1904. A memorial plaque hangs on the harbour wall. The plan was to make the entry to the harbour safer by dredging the bottom to clear the dangerous rocks lying there and to construct two piers. As a result the salt for curing could be more easily imported and the kippers could be shipped directly from the harbour rather than being transported by road, then rail. In 1910 whinstone shipments commenced. This led to a fierce altercation between the fishermen and the whinstone traders as they scrabbled for mooring places within the harbour.

The problem was eventually solved in a rather ingenious way. The whinstone was brought down from the quarry by an overhead rail system of wires and buckets and tipped into tall bins at the end of the south pier. It could then be poured into the holds of the waiting vessels, which didn't need to enter the harbour but could berth at the end of the pier. They could then complete the loading in 1 to 2 hours rather than occupy quay space for up to a day. A reluctant acceptance resulted. The export of whinstone ceased in 1938, considered no longer commercially viable. The iconic large concrete structure on the end of the south pier puzzles many a visitor. It was the base for the tall bins used for storing whinstone at the harbour. These bins were removed from their base at the beginning of World War II because they could have been landmarks for enemy aircraft.

Today Craster is considered one of the most picturesque fishing villages on the whole of the north-east coast – always a delight to paint. My wife, daughter and I lived here for a while and fell in love with the place and the people. One of the many highlights was putting to sea in the cobles helping to catch crab and lobster.

Craster is known world-wide for its kippers. The cobles are dragged up the beach on wooden rollers virtually to the door of the Kipper Sheds. The humble herring is then split, salted and then hung in rows to be smoked over a low fire sprinkled with oak chips and sawdust by the well-known Robson family, once our next door neighbours.

Sadly, like everywhere else along the coast, fishing is on the decline. There are few cobles surviving to carry on a great tradition.

R.W. Thornton

Howick

Howick pronounced Ho-wick is a small, attractive village between Craster and Boulmer, just inland from the sea, into which flows the Howick Burn from Howick Hall. Howick Hall, a Grade II listed building, is the ancestral seat of the Earls Grey. It was at one time the home of the Prime Minister – Charles, the 2nd Earl Grey, after whom the world famous tea is named.

The Earl Grey tea was specially blended by a Chinese mandarin for the 2nd Earl Grey to offset the taste of lime in the local water at Howick. Twinnings eventually came to market it and it has since sold world-wide. The Greys didn't register the trade mark and therefore unfortunately didn't receive a penny!

The port of Howick has belonged to the Grey family since 1319. A tower house once stood there but was demolished in 1780. It was described as 'a most magnificent freestone edifice in a square figure, flat roofed and embattled with a handsome court and gateway to the front'. The Hall which occupies the site today was built in 1782 by the Newcastle Architect, William Newton, and later was enlarged in 1809.

Lord Grey came to live here in 1801 and fathered sixteen children – 16 children, 15 or 10 depending on the research explored – shall we settle for numerous? This was by one wife and they all survived, an extraordinary achievement for those times. His father, 1st Earl Grey was a General who needed a 'good war' experience to advance his career. As a result he made his name in the American War of Independence when, during a surprise night attack, he ordered his men to remove the flints from their muskets – an unheard of procedure. This was to prevent them from being discharged accidentally and so alerting the enemy. Thereafter he was known as, "no-flint Grey". He also reintroduced marching in step on manoeuvres to move the troops more quickly, not used since Roman times.

An attractive path starts at the mouth of the Howick Burn, passes Howick Haven, on to the well known 'Rumbling Kern' and ends at the black Basaltic cliffs of Cullernose point some 120 ft. high. Here the mass of rock known as the Great Whinsill protrudes into the sea.

The winding path up the dene was a favourite walk of Charles, the 2nd Earl Grey, and he would walk every day here with his family. He was the best known of a distinguished family. A leading whig politician in the early 1800s before becoming Prime Minister in 1830. He introduced the Great Reform Bill of 1832, a huge step towards parliamentary democracy, against great opposition at that time.

The Bathing House is a very unusual and charming cottage in an idyllic and desirable location on the edge of the Northumberland coast. It commands panoramic views from every window and has a small sandy bay below. It was built in the early 19th century by the 2nd Earl Grey for his large family. His monument stands proudly at the top of Grey Street in Newcastle upon Tyne. On the rocks to the south east of the house, near a small sandy bay, iron pegs can still be seen that anchored the tents in which the children changed. Below them two bathing pools were hacked out of the rocks. The design of the house included a large upstairs sitting room where Lady Grey used to sit and watch the children bathe.

R.W. Thornton

Boulmer

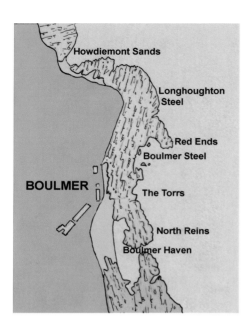

Boulmer is a tiny village on the North Sea Coast east of Alnwick. Despite its small size it can boast its own lifeboat station from which operates a lifeboat named "The Pentland Night". It is also home to R.A.F. Boulmer, one of the main search and rescue helicopter bases in the northeast. The history of Royal Air Force Boulmer began in 1940, when it was used as a decoy airfield to divert attacking German aircraft away from nearby R.A.F. Acklington, then an operational airfield. This involved aircraft and hangars made from wood and canvas. It was then reconstructed in 1943 as a Spitfire Training Unit.

The name Boulmer, pronounced 'Boomer', is thought to be a derivation of Bulemer from the old English bulan – mere meaning "bulls mere". This fishing village has been connected with the barony of Alnwick since the 1300s and many of the cottages are still part of the Duke of Northumberland's Estate. A row of pretty terraced cottages, once the homes of a number of fishermen, face onto a sandy beach where the sea virtually laps their front doors, presenting a magnificent, unspoiled view of this wonderful coastline.

Alongside the coastal cottages lies the local pub, "The Fishing Boat Inn", offering a welcome opportunity to rest, quench your thirst and soak up the peace and quiet of this idyllic spot. It must be said, however, that "The Fishing Boat Inn" had a dreadful past, going back many centuries. It was notorious as a centre for smuggling activities. Bootleggers came from all over Northumberland and the Borders in order to collect their contraband, which had arrived from the Netherlands and Scotland. On offer were illicit whisky, gin, tobacco, salt and many other goods. The landlord of the inn owned a smuggling lugger named "The Ides" that was moored in the harbour. It was armed and crewed by some twenty members. The lugger sailed out of the tiny harbour to meet up with vessels waiting out at sea to unload their contraband cargo. In the 1700s, one of the most well known smugglers was a gypsy called William Faa who lived miles away in a remote village in Scotland called Kirk Yetholm. A long way to come for a drink! The proof that some visitors travelled great distances is underlined by yet another frequent visitor to Boulmer, *Awd Bob Dunn*, who came with three horses, all the way from Rothbury. On his return he stored the illicit gin in spaces between the double walls of his farmhouse prior to selling it.

The ongoing debate regarding the melting of the polar ice caps and the consequent significant rise in global sea levels is of some real concern. The main painting of Boulmer indicates clearly that should such a catastrophe happen, a piece of history and much admired scenery will be washed away forever. Added to the woes, a major research project into coastal erosion has led to the cliffs at Boulmer being the most intensively measured set of cliffs on earth.

R.W. THORNTON

Alnmouth

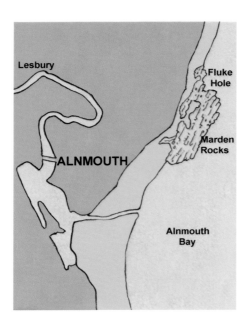

Perched upon a spit of land created by the sea and the river, Alnmouth nestles in one of the most attractive estuaries along the coast. It used to be pronounced and spelled Alemouth. The Roman legions building Hadrian's wall had a settlement in Alnmouth and used the harbour for the embarkation of troops. The village is purported to have been established as a seaport by William de Vesci of Alnwick Castle around 1150, an understandable move as the mouth of the River Aln provided a sheltered anchorage for fishermen and traders. The Normans 'laid out' the village in the 12th century and it quickly began to prosper. In 1207 Alnmouth was granted a Charter for a port and a market and was then considered to be the most important seaport between the rivers Tyne and Tweed.

Overlooking the sea is a steep, grassy slope known as Beacon Hill where traces of ancient camps lie buried beneath the turf. Here stood the Northern Church of St. Waleric. There was also a beacon (fire pans)

located here which were lit by chosen members of the village when news of impending raids by the Scotts came through. Border strife lasted here from 1293 till 1707. Trade continued to flourish, mainly involving grain which led to the village building a number of granaries. The 1750s saw the construction of the turnpike or 'corn' road from Alnmouth to Hexham. Ships were built at Alnmouth - the first vessel weighed 300 tons and was launched in May 1763. Ten ships at that time were owned by the port. A number of locally owned ships also used the port, bringing general cargo destined for Alnwick merchants.

One of the imports was guano (bird droppings). This was imported from the Chincha Islands of Peru and was used in the production of nitrogen fertiliser. When the guano ships came ashore the wind was obviously blowing inland and everyone was made aware of their arrival by the strong smell. The unpleasant task of unloading the cargo was often carried out by the girls of the village.

On Christmas Day in 1806 disaster struck. A violent storm blew with pouring rain. The river Aln was flooded as never known before or since, prompting it to change course, cutting off Beacon Hill and seriously damaging the church. The new harbour was formed

but was not as deep or navigable as the previous one. This made it difficult for ships to anchor and the port began to decline. The coming of the railways also created a significant drop in trade and the granaries were converted to houses.

Old Alnmouth had quite a reputation for smuggling and this was carried out 'with much boldness and success' according to one visitor. There were two types of smuggling. One where the contraband was landed on the beach from boats belonging to the fast sailing luggers out at sea, the other from cargo ships moored in the harbour where goods were sneaked ashore without paying duty. The contraband from the luggers was taken by the women, using ponies, to Rothbury. Another concern was the press gangs who would appear without warning, taking away all the men needed. The women left behind were less than pleased - well at least most of them! They chanted a song to warn their men folk to hide.

"Dance the tittery tan Margery
Dance the tittery tan
Here comes the tender
To take away our man"

R.W. THORNTON

Warkworth

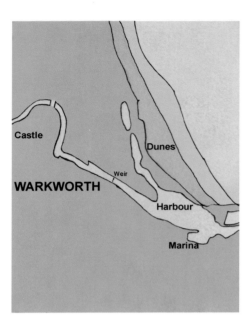

A n attractive small town built within the loop of the River Coquet about 1½ miles from the river mouth. It enjoys marvellous views to the east over the river and the sea to Coquet Island and is dominated by its Castle in which Shakespeare set his Henry IV. The first castle was built in 1140, a "motte and bailey affair" by Henry son of David I, King of Scotland. In 1332 it was given to Lord Percy of Alnwick by King Edward II, the first Duke of Northumberland, added a three storey keep on the original motte, creating a much grander building.

It is interesting to learn that from certain marks and peculiarities in the masonry the early castle could have been built by the same workmen employed to build the castles at Alnwick and Dunstanburgh.

The Percys remained at Warkworth until the 1500s. The family crest can still be seen on the Lion Tower. The most famous of the Percys was Harry, known as Hotspur, who was brought up here. He later became a hero in the Battle of Otterburn.

Warkworth is also known for its hermitage hewn out of solid rock above the river bank opposite the castle. Said to be the refuge of a certain St. Bartram who accidentally killed his own brother, it dates from medieval times and was last used in the 16th century. It is reached by climbing stone steps and entering an oratory hewn out of solid rock. Inside there is an altar, a lavatory, a pool and a small chapel, all within a chamber some twenty feet in length, seven feet wide and seven feet high. Apparently there was a small building outside for the preparation of food.

Warkworth has one of the few fortified bridges left in the country. It has an imposing fortified gatehouse and was constructed in 1379, helping to keep invading armies at bay. That didn't happen in 1174 when Warkworth was the site of a massacre. Despite taking refuge in the castle and pouring molten lead from its battlements, many of the villagers were killed by the Scottish Army. The bridge was pedestrianised when the new bridge opened alongside it in 1965.

To some, Warkworth could scarcely be called a harbour when viewed today. The Coquet is tidal to about a mile above Warkworth's bridge and the river may have served as a trading harbour from as early as the 12th century. The monks of nearby Brinkburn Abbey were granted the right in 1178 to manufacture salt from seawater near the mouth of the Coquet, where the town of Amble would later be built.

In the 16th and 17th centuries coal and grindstones were shipped out to sea along with salt, grain, coal and salmon and this continued until the 18th century. As far back as 1626, eight fishermen were said to reside in Warkworth. The building of Amble harbour in the mid 19th century brought about the demise of Warkworth as a harbour. This surely does give Warkworth Harbour some credibility.

R.W. Thornton

47

Amble

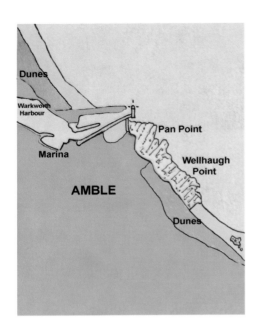

The town was built upon a peninsula and was first named Anna's Bill or Anna's Promontory - until 1985 it was know as Amble by the Sea.

There is evidence of a prehistoric burial ground on the links and at Gloster Hill signs of Roman occupation. Bones, urns and coins have all been found. In Norman times Amble was an agricultural hamlet and was part of the large estate of Robert de Mowbray. In 1090 he bestowed the manor on the monks of Tynemouth Priory. As far back as 1239 Henry III granted the monks a charter to export coal from Amble. This was an early indication of things to come.

It can be argued that the port of Amble largely owes its existence to the massive increase in demand for coal in the early 19th century. In 1837 an Act of Parliament appointed the Warkworth Harbour Commissioners to create a coal port by building quays, straightening the course of the river and providing berths for colliers.

In 1883 commissioners drew up breathtaking plans to create a National Harbour of Refuge across the mouth of the River Coquet. These would include a breakwater stretching 2 miles out to sea and linking up the southern side of the harbour with Coquet Island. Unfortunately, due to costs this imaginative scheme never materialised.

The coal industry boomed, helped by the opening of newly built railway lines. Coal was shipped to southern England and the continent in vast quantities. By the early 1920s, seven hundred vessels were loading nearly 750,000 tons of coal every year. I'm thinking about those living and working amidst the dust and noise! As well other industries graced the harbour but nowhere near the importance of the coal trade.

There is evidence of boat building in Amble taking place on the Braid. The first ship to be built in Amble was at the end of the 18th century when the "Chevington Oak" was constructed with timber from the nearby Chevington Woods. In 1840 Harrison's Boatyard was established and was well known for building traditional fishing cobles. Another firm, Messrs Leighton & Sanderson, built seven ships between 1851 and 1861 before closing down. A number of concrete vessels were built in the shipyard to replace lost ships during World War I. This sadly was a failure due to lack of technology at that time. Sea fishing of course has lasted over many centuries and thankfully still continues to some extent.

Today Amble is again a bustling harbour town and has seen recent positive developments. One is the award winning marina on the site of the former staithes. It was built in 1987, designed to berth 250 craft, offering a wide range of services and security.

The fishing industry survives albeit with fewer vessels as does a small marine industry, mainly concentrated around the construction and repair of yachts and other pleasure craft. Amble has its own lifeboat and a new D class boathouse and facilities was built in December 2002.

Amble holds the title 'Friendliest Port'. This goes back to the 1930s when the "R.M.S. Mauretania" was sailing past Amble, on her way to the breakers yard at Rosyth. The Amble Council sent a message to the ship saying, "Still the finest ship on the Seas". The "Mauretania" replied with "Greetings to the last and friendliest port in England". The word 'last' is significant and sad!

R.W. Thornton

49

Coquet Island

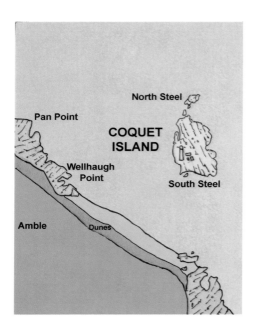

oquet Island is a small island with green pastureland of about 15 acres. It lies just over a mile off Amble on the Northumberland Coast. The island was well known as a place of peace and contemplation as far back as the 7th century. It was here that Abbess Elflaeda of Whitby visited St. Cuthbert in 684AD and eventually persuaded him to accept the Bishopric of nearby Lindisfarne.

It was in Norman times, however, that it became famous as a retreat of the much loved St. Henry of Coquet. St. Henry was a Danish nobleman who wished to found a hermitage in a quiet retreat and was allowed to live on the island by the monks of Tynemouth. He was widely accepted as a holy man and prophet and his advice was sought by rich and poor alike. Rather disrespectfully he was sometimes known as 'Henry the Hermit'. After his death he was enshrined in Tynemouth Priory.

The early monastery was extant in 1684AD and possibly destroyed around 800AD. A Benedictine cell was founded here and dissolved in 1593. Around this time a tower here was recorded as being a fortalice of Tynemouth Priory. The cell consisted of two domestic buildings with an attached chapel and a sacristy turret. In 1841 a new dwelling block was built, linking up with the tower - this was to form the base of the lighthouse in years to come.

Twenty years before the Coquet Lighthouse was built, the "Catherine" of Sunderland was wrecked on Steel Rock at the north end of the island. Nine men clung to the rigging throughout the night in sight of crowds who could do nothing to save them for want of a lifeboat – just one of the many wrecks involving the island over many years. Apparently this latest incident hastened the building of a lighthouse.

The lighthouse was built to the design of James Walker. The Victorian structure was built on the tower of the monastic cell already mentioned. The white square is of sandstone surrounded by a turreted parapet with walls over a metre thick. The dwelling houses were an integral part of the structure and it was here that the keepers lived during their period of duty. The lighthouse was completed in 1841 and cost Trinity House £3,268. The lighthouse is now operated automatically and stands 80 feet high. Its intermittent light is visible 14 miles offshore and an explosive fog signal gives extremely audible warning in thick weather off this very dangerous stretch of coast.

The first keeper appointed to the new lighthouse was one William Darling, the elder brother of Grace Darling. He was the second of her brothers to become a lighthouse keeper in the Trinity House Service. It is said that Grace developed a chill on a boat trip to visit her brother on Coquet Island in 1842. This apparently developed into the tuberculosis that killed her.

The Duke of Northumberland owns the island whilst the Royal Society for the Protection of Birds manages it as a bird reserve for its important sea bird colonies. The most numerous species is the Puffin, with over 18,000 pairs nesting in 2002. The island is most important, however, for the largest colony of the endangered Roseate Tern in Britain. Thanks to the conservation measures employed, notably the provision of nesting boxes to protect the nests from predatory gulls and bad weather, the number of breeding pairs had risen to 92 by 2005 but by 2009 had fallen to around 75. Egg theft could be contributing to this decline, but imprisonment and high fines may hopefully act as a deterrent.

R.W. THORNTON

51

Newbiggin-by-the-Sea

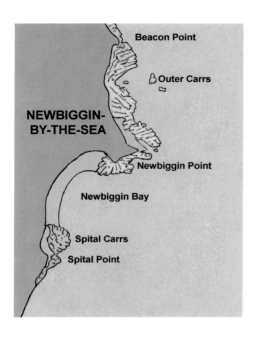

Newbiggin by the Sea was once a medieval grain port, then a mining village, and is now a fishing community with a fleet of traditional fishing cobles. It is an attractive seaside resort, with a large stretch of smooth sands edging the bay. The bay has benefited from one of the largest coastal protection schemes of its type ever to be undertaken on the north east coast, costing a massive £11 million. The problem was brought about by a lowering of the sea bed beneath Newbiggin Bay, thought to be the result of mining subsidence. This caused an increase in wave height entering the bay which swept away much of the sand, allowing erosion to the clay underneath. The result was a sandless, ugly bay posing a real threat to the sea walls, putting nearby property at risk.

The main element of the scheme was to import 500,000 tonnes of sand. This was brought by boat from the Lincolnshire coast near Skegness to replenish the beach and restore it to its former glory. In addition to the sand replenishment was the construction of a 200 metre long breakwater, 350 metres off shore in the middle of Newbiggin Bay. The regeneration scheme commenced in 2007 and is now complete. It has proved to be extremely successful and has restored Newbiggin by the Sea as a holiday attraction. It has brought about some controversy, however as the public are no longer allowed to walk their dogs along the beach.

Newbiggin by the Sea goes back a long way. The town was originally called South Wallerick. The Danes invaded in 875AD. The name Newbiggin derives from "new buildings or dwellings". It was a place of some importance: it had a pier and once equipped a ship for Edward II's fleet during his invasion of Scotland. In 1860 telegraph cables from Jutland in Denmark to Newbiggin by the sea were laid – a first. It was about this time that its importance as a fishing harbour began to decline. Large sailing boats from Scarborough and Hartlepool began to fish the waters off Newbiggin and Cullercoats, they were joined by the steam trawlers from North Shields, resulting in the Newbiggin fishermen settling for stake and net fishing in the summer and seaking labouring jobs on the shores of the Tyne for the rest of the year. The fisherwomen, in addition to some fishermen, also knitted the "ganseys" (jerseys) the men wore at sea. Each fishing village had its own pattern so when bodies were washed ashore they could be identified.

The village has the oldest operational lifeboat house in Britain - it was built in 1851. On December 19th 1904 lives were lost when the steamer "S.S.Anglia", feeling its way through mist and heavy seas while heading for Sunderland, ran aground at Needle Point off Newbiggin. The fishermen bravely put out to sea in their cobles before the lifeboat could be launched. The first coble to reach the stricken vessel was that of George Armstrong. An argument ensued when the captain of the "Anglia" refused help, despite the terrible danger they were all in, so that his ship could not be claimed as salvage. He thought it could be floated off at the next high tide. Eventually the coble capsized and seven local fishermen drowned.

A strikingly eye-catching feature of the bay is the old church of St. Bartholomew which stands to the north on Newbiggin Point. It is over 700 years old and still remains, some think, perilously close to the sea - it was damaged during the Second World War when mines exploded on the rocks and the seas have washed away part of the graveyard.

R.W. THORNTON

Cambois Bay

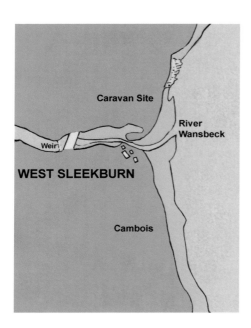

Caravan Site

River Wansbeck

Weir

WEST SLEEKBURN

Cambois

Cambois is a small seaside village stretching along the shoreline between the River Blyth and the River Wansbeck. The latter river rises above Sweethope Lough in an area known locally as "The Wanneys" and flows through Mitford, Morpeth and Ashington to the small but picturesque Cambois Bay before flowing out to sea. Here lie a small cluster of boats pulled up beyond the tide line, interspersed by a group of huts. Sadly the boats rarely put to sea but they and the huts provide a refuge for men who like to potter about, have a gossip and maybe escape for a few hours.

The name Cambois may have come from the word Cambion, meaning a house of trade or barter. There are seaports of the same name in Scotland and France. An alternative origin could be from pre-Anglo Saxon British language meaning "a bay". The pronunciation has varied over the years but locals insist that it is pronounced 'Cammus', very confusing for the visitor. The ancient history of the township centres round the north end and there is evidence of a chapel there as far back as 1204. There was 'scratch' coal mining in the 15th century and the first deep mine was sunk in 1783 but was closed shortly after. Some time later a rich seam was discovered amidst great excitement and it was anticipated that there would be employment for hundreds of men, giving rise to the building of a new pit village at the mouth of the Wansbeck above Cambois Bay. This village was built on the site of Browns' Farm, then the oldest farm house in the area. *Boca Chica* became well known as the nickname for a considerable part of Cambois. Apparently two seamen had served at the siege of Carthagena in South America. There the entrance to the harbour was known as Boca Chica or Little Mouth, neatly matching Cambois Bay. On their return they persuaded the residents to adopt the name.

When looking at the small bay it comes as a surprise to learn that quite large vessels managed to sail up the river. Cambois had a fair export of corn and a sizeable import of Norwegian timber, and limestone from Beadnell and Sunderland. This trade gradually declined until the river was brought to life again when the North Seaton Colliery opened in 1859 and keels began to load there. These keels, flat-bottomed boats, were then rowed to Blyth and on their return were berthed at Cambois Bay.

Across the mouth of the River Wansbeck, between Cambois and the North Seaton Estate, there was a stout cable to which a boat was attached by means of chains and an iron ring. It was a primitive yet efficient contraption, which allowed a ferryboat to be pulled back and forth across Cambois Bay. Known as "Wheatley's Ferry" or more locally "The Chain". The ferry ran across the bay to the north bank where the Ship Inn and the grain store were situated. Arriving from the Blyth side you would access the harbour down a time-worn track which led to a small, red tiled cabin at the water's edge. This little path is still known to the locals as the 'shute'. Here you would meet Mr. Robert Wheatley, the ferryman. Born in 1861 he was the son of Josiah Wheatley who had been a Master Mariner and owned the boats that plied the coal and grain trade as well as the keels berthed in the bay. He used to charge a penny a crossing and these were prosperous times for him, as the only alternative then was a wide and difficult detour on foot to 'plodge' across at low tide. Apparently Robert reacted very angrily when he saw people taking a detour to avoid using the ferry. Using a chain to pull the boat across would seem to require unusual strength, but he craftily used the tidal flow to achieve the task. Robert Wheatley's grandson still lives in one of the houses shown in the main painting. Sadly Cambois Colliery closed in 1968 and the village was demolished in the 1970s.

R.W. THORNTON

Blyth

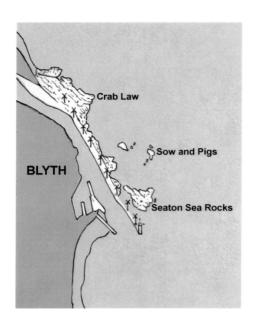

The port of Blyth is rich in history. Offshore rocks protect the pier that extends almost a mile into the sea north of the harbour. Here can be found the ore carrier terminal for unloading 'bauxite' aluminium ore, which is carried by train to the aluminium smelters at Lynemouth.

Upstream is the Cambois station and the huge wood framed coal staithes (West Staithes) that used to deliver coal to the waiting colliers from the renowned pits of Ashington, Bedlington and Newbiggin. For a brief period during the 20th century it shipped more coal than any other port in the whole of Europe. The oldest surviving coal-powered plant in the country, Blyth's 1965 station, capable of providing enough electricity for over 1,500 homes, was decommissioned in April 2000. Thousands watched the demolition of the famous massive chimneys.

In 1992 nine wind turbines were stationed on the east pier. Two of which were 548 ft. in height, the other two being 449 ft. – they are visible for many miles. More recently, in 2002, Blyth was host to the UK's first offshore wind farm when two wind turbines were erected.

In the early days Blyth was noted for the salt pans. Salt making was at one time the main industry. In the middle ages Blyth exported salt, coal and grain from its sheltered natural anchorage and by the end of the 17th century a harbour with stone quays had been constructed. It then claimed a piece of railway history with one of the country's earliest wagonways. The Plessey Wagonway was built to carry coal from the pits to the harbour by horse drawn wagons.

In the 18th century a programme of harbour improvements began, aimed at providing better coal handling facilities and included a lighthouse. The first coal-loading staithes were built in 1788 as well as the high lighthouse, which still survives. This development encouraged the growth of ship owning in Blyth, rising from 3 vessels in 1761 to 15 by 1789. The modern port was built by the Blyth Harbour and Dock Company, created in 1854. The Blyth Harbour Commission of 1882 further improved the port and the North Eastern Railway Company built huge wooden staithes for shipping out the coal from the extremely productive local pits. The South Harbour was built in 1899.

A new era dawned in 1841 when the SS Bedlington was built at South Shields. Steam-powered and specially built to take on board loaded wagons of coal, it cost £5,000. Salt manufacture ceased in 1875 due to heavy taxation but Blyth continued to grow. Shipbuilding was actively pursued with two shipyards, a large dry dock and a floating dock for vessel repairs. The Blyth Iron Shipbuilding Company, formed in 1883, built Britains first aircraft carrier, "H.M.S. Ark Royal" launched in 1914.

Whilst Blyth has recently been modernised there are a number of handsome buildings left: Bath Terrace, a late 18th century row of fine buildings and once owned by some of Blyth's wealthiest shipowners. Behind the terrace is the old "High Light", one of Blyth's oldest structures built in 1788 and claimed to be the oldest lighthouse in Northumbria. It was originally coal burning, then converted to oil/gas and finally electricity. Until 1985 the High Light was in use as a navigation aid in conjunction with the Lower Light, built in the harbour entrance.

Blyth was shattered by the collapse of the coal industry but it has fought back. The port still thrives, handling over 1.5 million tonnes of cargo annually and a number of liners berth here from around the world.

R.W. THORNTON

Seaton Sluice 1

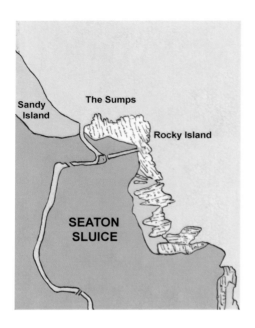

Seaton Sluice lies half a mile north of the village of Hartley. From as far back as 1236 salt pans were located in this area. The name 'Seaton' comes from the old English meaning a settlement (ton) by the sea.

The mouth of Seaton Burn has served as a natural haven for fishermen over the centuries. There were some 18 resident fishermen in 1626, and at that time only Spittal, Holy Island and North Shields could boast larger numbers on the Northumbrian coast. Five salt pan owners also made a living there at that time. Seams of coal were found in the area which would dramatically increase local prosperity. However, with its own haven unsuitable for coal shipping and Blyth being two miles away, too far to make overland carriage of coal economically possible, harbour construction became imperative. Yet it wasn't until around 1670 that a serious attempt was made to improve the haven at the mouth of Seatonburn.

The burn entered the sea in a north westerly direction, creating a problem. The mouth of the burn was very exposed and the entrance from the sea was oblique, making it difficult for ships to enter - once inside there was little space to moor.

Sir Ralph Delaval, one of the more sensible members of his family, decided to have a pier constructed at the east mouth of the burn. The pier consisted of square stones and was not cemented. As a consequence it didn't survive the very first gale. A second pier was built, this time cemented – it fared no better than the first. The third attempt was successful. The same stones were used but each was dovetailed to its neighbour, both horizontally and vertically with oak pegs. Even when they were lifted by huge waves they would sink down again into their original places. However, further problems arose - the haven began to silt up, possibly because the newly built pier was obstructing the movement of the river-borne silt out to sea. It was now being deposited, along with sand being swept in on the flood tide, onto the harbour bed. This led to Sir Ralph designing and building an ingenious mechanism to solve the problem – a sluice gate – hence Seaton Sluice.

R.W. Thornton

Seaton Sluice 2

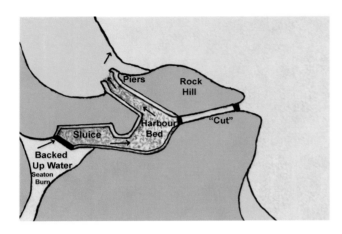

The sluice gate was situated near the present road bridge across the burn and was closed as the tide ebbed. This caused a 'back up' of water from the burn. When the harbour had emptied a horse and plough cleared the bed of rock, sand and silt. When the sluice was hauled up, the burn backwater raced into the harbour clearing even more debris, as it flowed into the sea. The system was very much admired and was widely visited - one was the famous 18th century engineer, John Smeaton.

Some 14 vessels used the harbour, as it now was, in 1685 and 56 cargoes, mainly coal and some salt where shipped out. However the tidal harbour was still far from ideal. Sometimes there wasn't enough water for a collier-brig to load completely within the harbour; it would be partially loaded and sail out to sea to have the remainder of its load topped up by keel. A costly venture. About this time a new industry began in the area, the manufacture of glass bottles, which needed to be exported by ship. This underlined the need for even further improvements to the harbour. A bold plan, for the time, was conceived. A 'cut' would be made from the mouth of the burn directly to the sea through the rocky headland in an easterly direction. Some undertaking! The 'cut' would have stop gates at each end and would serve as an alternative entrance channel to the harbour.

When both stop gates were closed it would act as a small 'wet dock' and also allow loading no matter what the state of the tide. Piers would protect the seaward entrance. The 'Cut' was officially opened in 1764, two years after the opening of the bottle works. 900 feet long, 30 feet wide and 52 feet deep it created 'Rocky Island' and to give access to the newly isolated buildings a drawbridge was built across the 'Cut'. A wooden footbridge now stands there. The absence of "passing places" caused some difficulties; another problem was the realisation that ships loaded to capacity could only get away at high tide. Despite this, in 1777 one hundred and seventy seven brigs sailed out of the harbour carrying 48,000 tonnes of coal. In the same year 1,740,000 bottles were produced. The bottles were sent down to the harbour via narrow gauge railways running through tunnels, which were used as air raid shelters during the Second World War. They were carried to London on 'bottle sloops' and on approaching the arches of old London Bridges they were able to lower their main mast to allow passage. Competition from other glassmakers proved too much and the bottle works closed in 1872.

Meanwhile increasing facilities at Blyth and the Port of Tyne were making profitable coal exports more difficult. This was exacerbated by the Hartley Pit disaster which spelt the end of the coal trade from Seaton Sluice. It became a quiet backwater used only by a few fishing cobles and pleasure vessels. Still a picturesque little harbour but with an outstanding history.

R.W. THORNTON

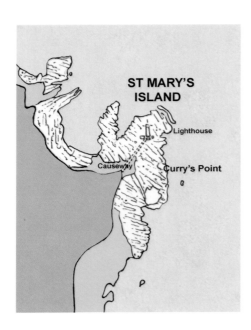

ST MARY'S ISLAND

Lighthouse

Causeway

Curry's Point

St. Mary's Island

St. Mary's Island is made of sandstone and can only be reached by a rocky causeway from the mainland, Curry's Point, at low tide. The island is dominated by the 126 ft. lighthouse built in 1898. It was probably the home of hermits in the early days of Christianity, similar to Coquet Island and the Farne Islands. The Viking invasion in 800AD would have certainly put a stop to the building of a settlement until after 1066. In 1090 the priory of Tynemouth was restored by Robert de Mowbray, the Norman earl of Northumbria. It is likely that soon after, a chapel dedicated to St. Helen was built on the island. The chapel was on the north side of the island and had a tower with an extra storey where a lantern was kept burning. It was initially known as the Lady Light, also known as St. Katherine's Light. The light was later wrongly ascribed to St. Mary and as a result the island became known as St. Mary's Island. It is also uncertain as to whether the light was used as a warning for shipping or its purpose was purely religious. Next to the chapel was a burial ground where monks and local folk were laid to rest. The traces of St. Helen's Chapel were destroyed when the lighthouse was built.

After the dissolution of the monasteries the island was known as Bates Island. It was owned by Thomas Bates, surveyor of Northumberland under Queen Elizabeth I in the 1580s. Again some misunderstanding occurred. The Ordnance Survey map spells it as Bait Island, the original surveyors wrongly thought that the name referred to the bait dug up by fishermen on the island.

In 1739 Michael Curry, a glass worker from Seaton Sluice, was hanged in Newcastle for the murder of Robert Shevil, landlord of the inn at Old Hartley. As was the custom then, the body was strung up from a gibbet within the sight of the crime and it still known today as Curry's Point. In 1799 the island was used to isolate Russian soldiers who had cholera while on a voyage south to face Napoleon. Those who died were buried on the island.

It will come as no surprise that smuggling was rife on the island. The deep, winding rocks on the north of the island are known as "Smugglers Creek". In 1722, Anthony Mitchell, Surveyor of Customs, was found dead near the creek, thought by many to have been murdered by two villains who used to "run" brandy. Contraband was hidden in haystacks along the links. 1855 saw the building of a cottage in front of the lighthouse by a fisherman called George Ewen. He had rented the salmon fishing rights in 1852 from Lord Hastings, his landlord, who supplied the building materials for the cottage. This was to be rented to the fishermen who used the island – a bothie with 2 rooms and thatched with bents (grass). In 1862 he turned the cottage into an inn called the "Freemasons Arms", known locally as the "The Square and Compass". Two extensions had been added to the cottage in 1861 prior to it opening as a pub, a barrel room and a washing room. During the building human remains were uncovered, probably those of a Russian cholera victim.

Before the lighthouse was built there were many wrecks, usually small fishing boats. The saddest occurred on Whitley Sands on New Years day 1861 when the "Lovely Nelly" from Seaham was driven on to rocks at Briardene during a blizzard. The fisherwomen from nearby Cullercoats pulled their lifeboat round the headland and all the crew were saved except for the little cabin boy named Tommy who was too frightened to jump from the rigging. An oil painting called "The Women" by John Charlton hangs in the Laing Art Gallery in Newcastle and commemorates their courage.

The lighthouse remained operational until 1984. Visitors can climb the 137 steps inside the lantern room to enjoy spectacular views along the coast in

R.W. THORNTON

Whitley Bay

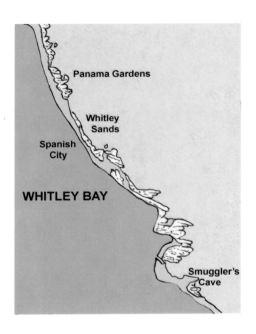

<M>any centuries ago early settlers occupied dry open pastureland on the coast two miles north of the river Tyne. They gave it the name of White Lea or Whitley. This name lasted until the 1890s, by which time the confusion of the name with Whitby in Yorkshire caused widespread misdirection of mail. The final straw came when an ex-resident died in Edinburgh and was about to be interred in Whitby when the mistake was discovered. The body was transported back to Whitley for a proper burial. As a result residents in Whitley were asked to choose a new name, the most popular choice was Whitley Bay and this was adopted.

Whitley Bay in the 18ᵗʰ century was a bustling place due to the coal, salt and limestone exports but relapsed into a quiet country village when these activities declined. By 1821 the village had a pleasing rural appearance with attractive houses and by 1861 Whitley Bay got its very own railway station in the centre of the town.

This was linked to the North Tyne Loop railway line in 1882, connecting the coastal villages to Newcastle. This new development brought about changes on a massive scale. Entrepreneurs now realised the potential of this beautiful shoreline as a future mecca for holidaymakers and building operations developed on a massive scale. The picturesque little village gradually disappeared and a small seaside resort grew up from its ashes. 'The Blackpool' of the north east coast was born. In its early years it was visited by the residents of Newcastle upon Tyne and adjoining districts. Increased travelling facilities rapidly widened the intake of visitors who came to enjoy the sea air. The climate was described as being extremely bracing, invigorating, strengthening and vitalising (no mention of temperature!). For many years it was particularly popular with the residents of Glasgow, who decamped en masse to enjoy their summer holiday fortnight.

In 1972 the Local Government Act meant that the town was no longer governed by its local borough council. Some saw this as bringing about a loss of civic pride, resulting in a decline in appearance and lack of development. Whitley Bay was famous for its permanent seaside fairground the 'Spanish City' where generations of youngsters throughout the years

in search of amusement have entertained themselves and their future families. Its iconic dome will be remembered by many. Sadly, along with other areas, it fell into disrepair following the closure of the theme park in the 1980s.

Today Whitley Bay is enjoying a dramatic regeneration scheme. The most welcome aspect is the redevelopment of the Spanish City site – first built in 1912. Its function will not be an amusement park but rather a Centre for Culture. There is a new skateboard park, childrens' play park and a swimming pool that has undergone refurbishment.

The seaside resort of Whitley Bay has a unique atmosphere at weekends and bank holidays where young people come from far and wide to sample its nightlife. This has brought about conflicting views from the residents. Some are not happy with the disruption, whilst others see it as a source of revenue and an enlivenment of the sea front.

R.W. THORNTON

Cullercoats

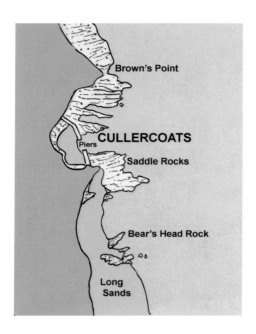

Cullercoats is sandwiched between Tynemouth and Whitley Bay. It was a tiny industrial and fishing harbour with stone piers and a safe, sheltered sandy beach.

Historically the village depended on fishing. There was also local coal mining in what were called bell pits; here the coal seams were shallow and easily accessible. The coal was used to fire salt pans and was also exported from the harbour - a pier had been constructed for this purpose. The coal was carried from the pits to the harbour by a horse-drawn wagonway.

Houses were built on the point overlooking the sea - residents included a blacksmith, carpenter, two Master Mariners ensuring a combination of talent and wealth – important people for the growth of Cullercoats. Cliff House, also known as Bank Top House, was built in 1768 by Captain Armstrong, a Customs Officer.

Ironically he became involved with smuggling, allowing his cellar, along with a secret tunnel leading to the cliffs, to accommodate contraband goods and to hide the smugglers themselves. Once discovered, he was dismissed, but the smuggling continued.

The salt industry declined and the growth of the railways led to coal shipments being relocated to better ports e.g. the Tyne and Amble. This left fishing as the main industry. As a result two piers were built on either side of the harbour to provide increased shelter for the many cobles sailing from the harbour. In 1749 it was named "the best fish market in the north of England". It now took on the trappings of an early seaside holiday resort for the 'well off' who enjoyed bathing. This may have been encouraged somewhat when, in December 1805, a cask of gin was washed ashore and consumed on the spot by those lucky enough to be nearby. Apparently a great number of people were left lying totally drunk on the beach. I wonder what happened when the tide came in?

In 1848, a coble taking a pilot to a ship anchored further out at sea capsized with the loss of all on board. In response the local landowner, the Duke of Northumberland, funded the setting up of an R.N.L.I. lifeboat station. Then followed an even worse disaster costing 20 lifeboat members their lives. This prompted the Duke to sponsor a competition to design

a self-righting lifeboat. "The Percy" was built at the Duke's expense and delivered to Cullercoats in 1852. The Brigade House and watchtower were later added above the harbour. The Brigade House was built for the Cullercoats Life Brigade, which was formed in 1865. They were on duty in the stormiest of weather throughout the year and the building provided much needed protection. The harbour is also home to the Dove Marine Laboratory.

We dare not leave Cullercoats without mentioning their famous "Fishwives" – a legend in their own lifetime. They were instantly recognisable by their 'uniform'. The heavy dark blue skirts had numerous tucks and it is said that you could calculate how well off the fisherwife was by the number of tucks. The pleats in the heavy skirts were said to allow for steady growth. A white, cotton pinny (pinafore) was worn to protect the skirt when gutting fish, it had a money pocket fastened about the waist under the pinny. A brooch often decorated their blouse and a shawl and neckerchief were also worn. Under the skirts were worn bright red flannelette underskirts and also bloomers in white. All of this was topped off with a black straw bonnet. She would trudge along the streets with a heavy creel of fish on her shoulders shouting, "Whe'll buy me feesh". When the local market was poor they would trudge the 10 miles to Newcastle carrying their fish with them.

R.W. THORNTON

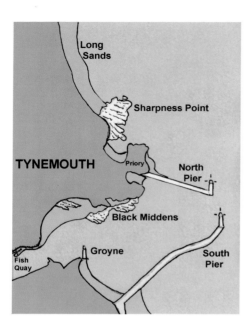

Tynemouth

Tynemouth stands at a spot where the Tyne enters the sea and embraces two distinct areas. One is the industrial background of North Shields and the other one of the most sought after seaside resort on the North East Coast.

The seafront of Tynemouth with its handsome promenade, history, and stretches of golden sand has attracted many visitors over the years. Tynemouth Longsands is a wide, sandy beach that stretches into the distance and has become well known for surfing. King Edward Bay beach is a smaller, staid, secluded beach that nestles under the Priory. Such was the reputation they attracted such famous people as Lewis Carroll, Dante Gabriel Rossetti and Charles Dickens who apparently was overcome by a wave and soaked to the skin - something to write home about!

The best view of Tynemouth, in my opinion, is from the beach at South Shields across the estuary. The rocky headland offers a dramatic silhouette of the Priory, Castle and Watchtower. These have been gazed upon by mariners throughout the years with mixed emotions, dependent on whether they were returning home or embarking on yet another long sea voyage. Beneath the Priory, standing on a 50 foot pillar is the tall statue of Admiral Collingwood. Hatless, he gazes out to sea. Below him are four of the actual cannons from his ship "the Royal Sovereign". In this vessel he led the British fleet into action at Trafalgar. He engaged the French for a full hour before the rest of the British fleet arrived. Collingwood is buried alongside Nelson in St. Paul's Cathedral.

Below Tynemouth lie the notorious Black Middens, a stretch of rocks that have claimed countless lives over the years. After the sinking of the steamship "Stanley" along with the loss of 26 lives in 1869 it was decided enough was enough. The people of Tynemouth formed a Volunteer Life Brigade, the first in the country. The great piers were built and opened in 1895, dramatically increasing harbour safety. It is interesting to note that the River Tyne was responsible for the world's first lifeboat and the country's first Volunteer Life Brigade – underlying how dangerous the river entrance was at that time.

No trace remains of the first monastic building to be constructed on the headland around the 7th century. During one of the frequent Danish raids it suffered appalling losses. In 865 all of the nuns sheltering there were massacred. The Castle was built later when the military of that time realised the significance of its defensive position. However the ruins of the Priory are still an impressive sight. It was rebuilt in 1100 as a cell of St. Albans. Legend has it that the monks of St. Albans who "misbehaved" were exiled to Tynemouth Priory to help them see the error of their ways. One such luckless resident penned the following heart-breaking missive back to his colleagues. "Our home is confined to the high rock and is surrounded by sea on every side. Day and night the waves break and roar and undermine the cliffs. Thick sea frets roll in, wrapping everything in gloom. Dim eyes, hoarse voices, sore throats are a consequence. Spring and summer never come here…" If ever there was a strong incentive for the St. Alban monks to behave, surely this must have been it!

R.W. Thornton

The Tyne to the Tees

"*I love - oh how I love to ride,*
On the fierce, foaming, bursting tide!
When every mad wave drowns the moon,
Or whistles aloft the tempest tune!
And tells how goeth the world below,
And why the south-west blast doth blow."

from "The Sea" by Bryan Waller Procter (1787 - 1874)

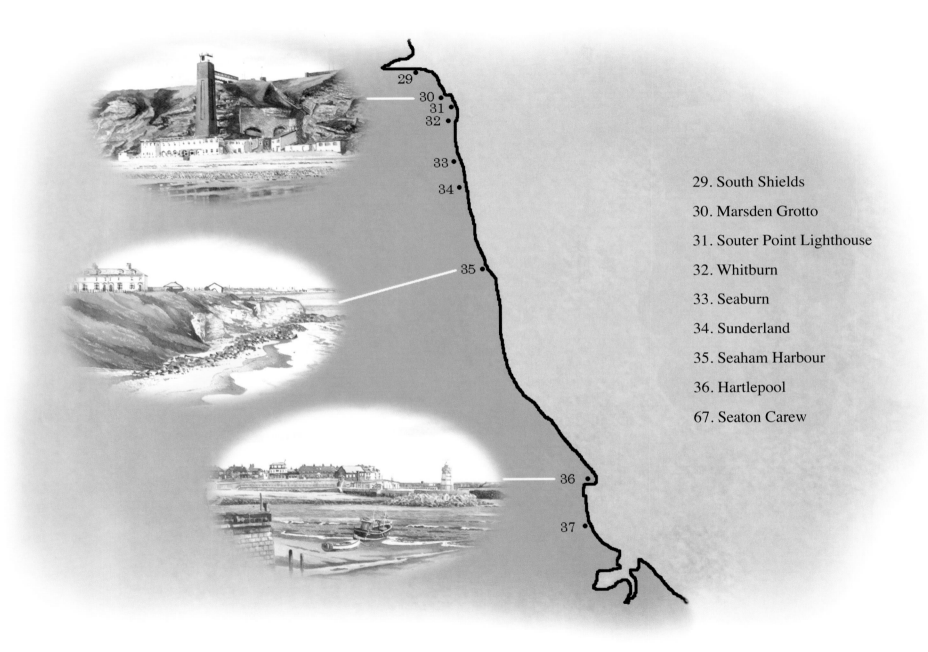

29. South Shields

30. Marsden Grotto

31. Souter Point Lighthouse

32. Whitburn

33. Seaburn

34. Sunderland

35. Seaham Harbour

36. Hartlepool

67. Seaton Carew

South Shields

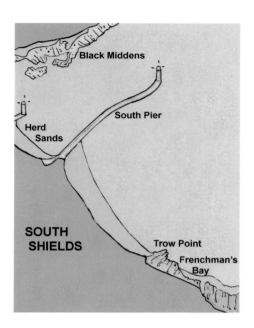

South Shields is situated on a peninsula, where the River Tyne meets the North Sea. It has six miles of coastline and is dominated by two massive piers at the mouth of the Tyne. Early inhabitants of the area were the Brigantes, a strong and fiercely independent ancient British tribe. It was they who apparently named their settlement Caer Urfa, meaning "town on the rocks", Caer being a fortified place. In 80AD the Romans arrived led by Agricola who built a large fort, Arbeia, overlooking the mouth of the River Tyne. Abandoned around 400AD, it has been magnificently restored and is now a museum. In 1100 the Normans built St. Hilda's Church in the town's market place. The church remains one of the oldest in Great Britain.

Salt panning along the Tyne began in 1499 and achieved major importance with as many as 200 salt pans working in the vicinity of Holborn. When all the pans were working, visitors likened it to Dante's Inferno. The pollution was dreadful and it was said that the pall of smoke could be seen from as far away as the distant Cheviot Hills. By the 1600s fishing vessels would arrive in their hundreds and load salt for preserving their catches. The Mill Dam, which used to be a tributary on the south side of the river, acted as a demarcation line. Those living on the east were known as "fishers" (fishermen) and those to the west "panners" (salt makers).

The first glassworks was established in 1650 by Isaac Cookson and was so successful that by 1827 there were eight glassworks in operation. Coal mining and chemical manufacture also increased in importance and South Shields had the largest alkali works in the world which opened in 1822. Alkali could be mixed with other substances to produce soap, alum and also glass. The area was noted for glass making as far back as the 17th century and by 1845 the town was producing more plate glass than anywhere else in England. For centuries both North and South Shields fought the Newcastle monopolists who did all in their power, by fair means or foul, to stifle trading and industrial initiatives by what they regarded as "river mouth upstarts". Finally in 1850 it was forced to relinquish some of its powers over the river and its trade when Parliament passed The Tyne Navigation Act. This left the door open for further massive development.

In the 18th and 19th centuries the demand for coal was quite startling, and pits were opened up, particularly around the River Tyne where coal was readily accessible.

The mouth of the Tyne was notoriously dangerous. On occasions it was possible to wade across the harbour at low tide, and has claimed hundreds of lives over the years with ships running aground frequently. In 1854 work was begun to build a north and south pier to protect the harbour. A railway was constructed to carry the stones to the South pier. They were not completed until 1895, the North Pier being 2,959 feet long and the South Pier 5,170 feet long. The building of the piers presented a further problem; the sand on Littlehaven Beach was now flowing up the Tyne on the incoming tides. To prevent this the Groyne Pier was built in 1882.

Local man William Wouldhave designed the world's first self-righting lifeboat in 1790. The world famous artist L. S. Lowry spent frequent periods in nearby Seaburn and painted a number of works in South Shields.

I was born in South Shields, and as a young lad of ten remember taking my Father's bike from the back yard, along with a sack with a shovel inside, and pushing it nearly 2 miles to what we called "The Little Beach". I had to push it because it was very large and very heavy and I was too small to ride. On reaching the beach, in those days literally covered in sea coal, I filled the sack, struggled to lie it over the crossbar, and panted and puffed my way home - largely uphill I remember!

R.W. THORNTON

73

Marsden Grotto

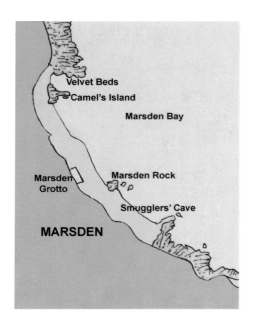

Velvet Beds
Camel's Island
Marsden Bay
Marsden Grotto
Marsden Rock
Smugglers' Cave
MARSDEN

The coast between South Shields and Sunderland is magnificent with a mixture of golden sands and rocky cliffs protruding into the sea at Lizard Point and the impressive Marsden Bay. Marsden Rock standing in the bay between the sea and the cliff is certainly eye-catching. It is some 130 feet high with many kinds of sea birds seeing it as an ultra safe sanctuary for them to build their nests, their incessant shrieking often drowning the sound of the waves pounding against the base of the rock. The Rock is the same height as the nearby cliffs and at one time was obviously part of them. Because of its isolated position the rock was attacked by the sea on both sides and a hole was worn right through forming a natural arch. In 1986 it finally gave in to the centuries of pounding by the waves and collapsed leaving two small stumps of rock, one of which proved unstable and was demolished in 1997. The rock is a limestone, greyish-yellow in colour. At Marsden you will find a fascinating collection of natural arches, sea stacks and caves.

Not unexpectedly Marsden Bay, with its many caves, was a popular spot for smugglers. But the most unusual character to haunt this coast must be "Jack the Blaster", the first person known to live in the caves. He was originally a miner in Allendale and moved to Marsden in 1782 to work in the local limestone quarry. Allendale is a significant distance from Marsden - how did he know about the quarry? How did he find his way there and how did he travel? From a small cave in the cliffs he blasted his way to a bigger one. It would be interesting to know what he used for such blasting! The bigger cave became a home for Jack, who was thought to be 80 year old then, and his wife. They were known for their eccentric behaviour and it wasn't long before people began to visit the curious pair in their bizarre home. They used the steep zig-zagging steps which he had dug out of the cliff face to reach the "dwelling". He wasn't that daft however, as he started selling food and drink to his various visitors. It has been suggested that he became involved with the smuggling community. Jack's grotto must have been a heavenly place for tired smugglers to escape the cold, feed their hunger and enjoy a tankard or three.

The next resident of the Grotto was a Peter Allan. He had the energy and the imagination to make it into a more accessible and sophisticated enterprise. Having also worked in the local limestone quarry he had some knowledge of the skills required for further development. The idea of living in a cave with fantastic sea views whilst at the same time providing refreshments for the general public, many of whom flocked to the beach during the summer months, greatly appealed to him. He eventually succeeded in creating a two storey cave which included a kitchen and, above of all things, a ballroom. He was successful in turning Jack's cave into an inn, a commendable feat.

In 1848 a dispute over the land resulted in Allen being charged rent for his home and inn. He became very miserable and sulked until he died the following year. His wife and their 8 children ran the business successfully until 1865 when the cliff face collapsed resulting in considerable damage. They saw through the reinforcement to prevent further damage but eventually left in 1874. Various companies set up business in the Grotto, refurbishing the interior and outside buildings. It was Vaux Breweries who installed the lift and used the Grotto for over a century. Naturally there has to be a ghost. The most popular is a smuggler who "grassed" on his mates to H.M.Customs. His friends hanged him in a nearby cave called "Smugglers Hole" and it is said his wails can still be heard. Paranormal investigators claim they have found no less than seven separate tortured souls. That's the spirit!

R.W. Thornton

Souter Lighthouse

The lighthouse is located on Lizard Point at Marsden, but takes its name from Souter Point, located a mile to the south. This was originally the intended site but it was felt that Lizard Point afforded better visibility. The Souter name was kept to avoid any possible confusion with the then recently built Lizard Lighthouse in Cornwall.

Between South Shields and Sunderland lies a dangerous underwater reef called Whitburn Steel or Stile. In one year alone, 1860, there were 20 shipwrecks. It is said that the locals used to use false lights to lure the vessels on to the rocks so that they could steal the cargo. It was considered the most dangerous coastline in the country with an average of 44 shipwrecks for every mile. It was decided to build a lighthouse. Designed by James Douglass and opened in 1871, Souter Point Lighthouse was the first in the world to use electricity. The 800,000 candle power light was generated using carbon arcs and could be seen for up to 26 miles. It flashed a white light which lasted for 5 seconds every 30 seconds. The electricity was generated using a steam engine.

No doubt the lights were greeted with great acclaim but the same cannot be said of the foghorns. They were switched on when visibility was below 2 miles or when the Shields and Sunderland Piers could not be seen. The foghorn, reputed to be the loudest in Britain, could be heard as far north as Whitley Bay, as far south as Sunderland and for several miles inland as far as Jarrow. It meant sleepless nights for local residents. Apparently the lighthouse keepers were paid an extra 2d an hour "noise money". The lighthouse was decommissioned in 1988, but continued to serve as a radio navigation beacon until 1999 when it finally closed. The lighthouse today is owned by the National Trust and is open to the public; the lighthouse's engine room, light tower and keeper's living quarters are all on view. But beware, the lighthouse is said to be haunted.

Limestone had been quarried at Marsden for many years. The stone was used in local notable buildings, including Whitburn windmill nearby. Just inland from the lighthouse can be seen a set of limekilns. These kilns were built in the 1870s to take advantage of a nearby colliery which provided fuel for burning the limestone to make quick-lime which was used to make cement and concrete. This was important for the steel and chemical industries. They were 'large ovens' - layers of limestone and coal were put in the top and burnt slowly. The resulting quicklime was taken out at the bottom and loaded into railway wagons and taken to the docks at South Shields. The rail line also brought in coal from the colliery at Whitburn to fire the kilns and hereby hangs a tale.

The green fields to the north of the lighthouse were once the home of a thriving village called Marsden Village. It began in 1874 to provide accommodation for the miners in Whitburn Colliery. There were 135 houses in all, accommodating some 700 people. In the 1950s cliff erosion was threatening the village which was in danger of slipping into the sea. People were moved out to Whitburn and surrounding areas. The village was then completely demolished. Today there is no trace of it and the area is managed by the National Trust.

In 1879 a mineral railway line was opened to transport miners to and from South Shields to Whitburn Colliery. For cheapness the carriages and rolling stock were bought from various Rail Companies. Because of the mixture of wagons, the train was extremely noisy and became known as the "Marsden Rattler". The last service ran in 1953 and was crowded with passengers to wish it an affectionate farewell.

R.W. THORNTON

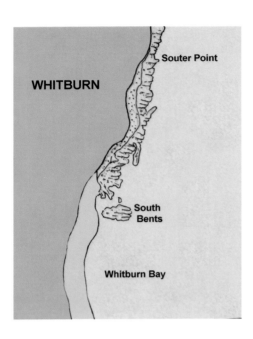

WHITBURN

Souter Point

South Bents

Whitburn Bay

Whitburn

Whitburn was probably a Saxon settlement and it is thought that the name came from the burial place of Hwita – a Saxon chief hence Hwita Byrgen. An alternative version is from the Old English Hwit (white) and bere-oern (barn).

From about 1700 up to the beginning of the 20th century Whitburn was a village with a rectangular layout. Inland lay farmsteads and on the shore were fishermens' cottages. This area was called The Bents, named after the sturdy grass growing at the bottom of the cliffs. The Bents, whilst part of Whitburn, kept themselves strictly apart and even had their own pub to drink in, "The Board", run by Bill Prior who was also a fisherman. At that time there were 12 cottages and 2 farms. Some of The Bents cottages existed in the time of the Napoleonic Wars, when many parts of the coast were fortified in anticipation of a French Invasion. Additional buildings were built on The Bents for troops to live in so they could repel "Boney's Soldiers".

There was no coast road until 1880. Coal and heavy goods were brought in by sea to The Bents and loaded onto carts to be trundled up to the village. Whitburn at the time was largely a self-sufficient community, mainly because of its farming and fishing.

Superstition has always played a large part in fishermens' lives all over the world. The story is told of a Whitburn fisherman, one of a crew of four, who set out from The Bents. As they rowed they heard a donkey braying on the cliff tops and the fisherman demanded that his colleagues return him to the shore immediately. The braying of a donkey is a sure sign of trouble at sea! His scornful companions reluctantly did as he wished and put back to sea again. As you might guess, a severe storm arose and the three men in the boat were never seen again.

Whitburn got its first lifeboat in 1830 which was stationed at The Bents. It was in service for 29 years and saved 139 lives. The lifeboat station was closed in 1918. The Whitburn Volunteer Life Brigade, formed in the 1840s, excelled during its existence, saving countless lives. The men were mainly from Whitburn, helped from time to time by other volunteers along the coast nearby. They were the first in the world to use a rocket type of apparatus eventually called

the Breeches Buoy. This was a round lifebelt inside which sit a pair of canvas shorts, so with the belt round your waist your legs dangle through the holes. It was invented by Captain Carte. In 1842 "The SS Cato" was driven onto the rocks near Souter Point. Lines were fired out to the ship but unfortunately there were no instructions and none of the crew knew how to use the apparatus. They lashed themselves to parts of the vessel that had escaped the breaking up. Thankfully they were rescued next day by boat. Despite its initial lack of success it must be remembered that the 'rocket line' saved countless lives around the world – well done Whitburn!

Sadly fishing declined over the years and Whitburn ceased to be a fishing harbour. Whitburn still, however, retains village customs handed down throughout the years. One of Whitburn's specialities is the "Loving Cup" or sometimes called the "Whitburn Hotpot". The brew originated as a drink to celebrate weddings at the Parish Church and was offered to the bride and bridegroom at the church door. Provided they were both from Whitburn, the drink was to ensure future happiness. It is said that the contents were mulled ale, rum, whiskey, sherry and spices. I wonder how they made it down the aisle!

R.W. THORNTON

79

Seaburn

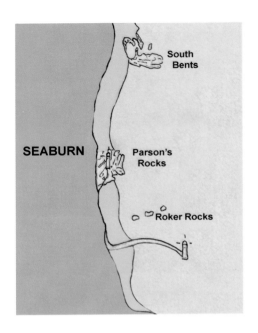

S eaburn was known as Sea Lane at the start of the 20th century. In 1918 a promenade and seating had been constructed above the beach. Seaburn, because of its lovely stretch of clean sand, quickly became a popular resort for holidaymakers. As a result tent and deckchair hire prices soared. The Sunderland Echo called for an end to the monopoly and in 1934 the Corporation took over control of the beaches. They bought 300 tents and 2,000 deckchairs. The tents were two shillings per session and deckchairs twopence per session. A season ticket for a tent cost five shillings – quite a bargain!

A plan was produced in 1934 for the construction of a concert and dance hall and in 1939 Seaburn Hall was officially opened. The building soon became extremely popular throughout the northeast for entertainment where some of the top artistes of that time performed. The dance hall could accommodate 1,000 dancers at any one time. Sadly over the years the building was allowed to deteriorate and became an eyesore, much to the annoyance of the Seaburn residents who regarded it as the centre of the resort - it was demolished in 1982.

After World War II the beach was opened to the public again when the army removed the swathes of barbed wire placed there to repel German invaders. Gradually Seaburn progressed as a seaside holiday resort. In the 1960s the sea front was vastly improved by the introduction of attractive 'super kiosks', lawns and flowerbeds. The kiosks became very popular selling toffee apples, 'willicks' with a pin to eat them, candy floss etc. It is reputed that the famous fortune teller Gypsy Rose Lee worked from one of the kiosks. The story goes she was concerned about overnight "break-ins" and wanted to buy a dog to protect the premises. Surely she could have foretold such an incident! By this time Seaburn boasted a fairground, miniature railway, boating pool, 9 hole miniature golf course and was becoming ever more popular.

For many years the name Notarianni dominated the resort. They were famous for their ice cream and eager customers queued year after year to sample what was on offer. The ice cream parlours were a meeting place for young couples prior to a visit to the local dance hall, the fair or the 'pictures'.

However, the 1970s saw the beginning of a decline. Seafront habits throughout the country were changing as local families travelled abroad in search of more reliable weather. The amusement arcade crashed with massive debts. The fairground became shabby and forlorn; the promenade became neglected with broken seats and bent railings. Things did not look well and the future uncertain. To make things worse the 'Big Dipper', a well-known landmark, which had dominated the skyline at Seaburn for 15 years, was suddenly closed in 1970 after a fatal accident. The Dipper was then demolished.

Today Seaburn is back on the up. The old Seaburn Hall was given a £4 million revamp and today is known as the "Swallow Hotel" run by Marriott.

The popular Sunderland International Air Show is held on the coast at Seaburn, the largest free airshow event held in Europe. The show lasts for two days and is aimed at all ages with a wide variety of aircraft on display.

Sunderland's famous annual 'Boxing Day Dip' is held on the beach at Seaburn. Hundreds of brave locals plunge into the icy cold sea – no matter what the weather – snow, ice, rain or fog. To prepare them for their ordeal the local fire brigade showers the dippers with freezing water from hosepipes before they enter the sea. This is done to raise money for needy charities.

R.W. THORNTON

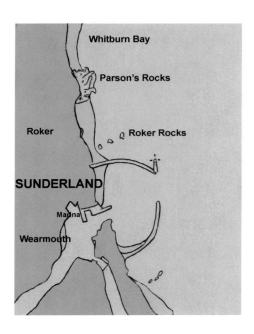

Sunderland

The port of Sunderland is situated on both sides of the mouth of the River Wear. As early as 1100 a small fishing village existed on the southern mouth of the river – the modern day Hendon. The name Sunderland is thought to come from Soender-land, soender or sunder meaning to part. This could refer to the river which splits the city in two. On the north side of the river lies St. Peter's Church, one of the most important sites of early Christianity in the country. Benedict Biscop founded the tiny Saxon Church in 674AD.

Until the 16th century Sunderland was merely a small port used by a few fishermen but all this was about to change. During the years of the Civil War (1642–1651), Sunderland backed parliament against the Newcastle Royalists. Up to this time Newcastle had a huge monopoly on the export of coal, now this had gone and Sunderland could move into this very lucrative trade. We can see how the Newcastle v Sunderland

soccer rivalry could have begun. However the Wear estuary was a mess, choked with sand, mud and river debris with two narrow channels that were difficult to navigate. This called for immediate action. In 1717 the River Wear Commissioners were formed to improve the river and the port. Extensive harbour works were carried out directed at the rapidly expanding coal trade and the increasingly important shipbuilding and repair industry. The north river channel was blocked and the south channel was dredged to increase the depth and flow of water. In 1723 work started on a south pier, which proved very successful, and as a result coal exports doubled between 1750 and 1790. A north pier was built in 1797.

Coal mines were opened up throughout the area and soon matched the collieries along the Tyne and Tees. One owner of a new deep mine is reputed to have said, "we'll go on until we sink down to Hell and then if we don't get coal we'll get cinders". The coal was brought from the pit in tubs to the riverside staithes and loaded into keels, flat-bottomed boats capable of carrying 20 tonnes of coal. They were rowed out to sea-going colliers anchored outside the harbour where the cargo was transferred by hand. A back-breaking task!

As coal production increased, there grew a need for more keels and colliers and this is the start of Sunderland becoming one of the world's most famous shipbuilders. By 1857 Sunderland, along with the

River Tyne shipyards, was responsible for one in three ships launched around the world. An incredible achievement! During the Second World War half of Britain's merchant ships came from the Wear.

In October 1831, Sunderland, a main trading port at the time, became the first British town to be struck with the 'Indian cholera' epidemic. Sunderland was put under quarantine and the port blockaded, but in December that year the disease had spread to Gateshead and from there it quickly made its way across the country, killing an estimated 32,000 people.

The Wearmouth Bridge was built in 1796. It was the second iron bridge to be built. At the time of building, it was the biggest single span bridge in the world. Further up the river is the Queen Alexandra Bridge, built in 1910. When St. Peter's Church was built in 674AD, French craftsmen were brought in to build the church in stone, (most buildings at that time were constructed of wood) and glaziers to make the earliest English glass - probably forerunners of the glassmakers in the area. Visitors at the National Glass Centre can see modern glassblowing techniques and gain a comprehensive history of the glassblowing throughout the years. The roof is made of clear glass panels some 30 ft. above the harbour and is part of the tour walkway. Not for the fainthearted!
The Sunderland Empire is known worldwide and continues to attract top entertainment stars.

Seaham Harbour

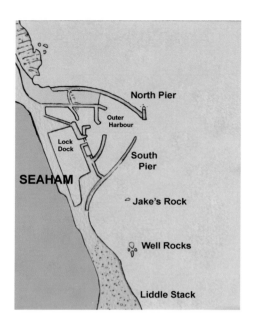

T oday Seaham Harbour has a population of 22,000. It is a town of rebirth after the disastrous collapse of the coal industry. It has fine beaches, once covered in coal waste but now restored. This is due to the 'Turning the Tide' project of 2002.

One of Seaham Harbour's best-known visitors was the poet Lord Byron. He came in 1814 when Seaham was a small farming community housing the 11th century parish church of St. Mary, reputed to be one of the 20 oldest surviving churches in the UK. Seaham Manor House, the home of the Sir Ralph Millbanke and his family, was his destination. Byron's marriage to their daughter Anne Isabella was short lived. He began writing his Hebrew Melodies at Seaham but did not like the place. Byron wrote to a friend "Upon this dreary coast we have nothing but country meetings and shipwrecks; and I have this day dined on fish, which probably dined upon the crews of several colliers lost in the late gales".

In 1821 the Millbankes sold Seaham Hall and Estate to Charles Stewart, 3rd Marquess of Londonderry and his wife, Frances Anne Vane Tempest. They added two wings to the Hall and extended and enclosed the grounds. In 1922 the Londonderrys moved away from the Hall and five years later gave it to Durham County Council for use as a sanatorium. For some fifty years valuable research was carried out on chest diseases until it was closed in 1978. Today it has become one of the best-known quality hotels in the country with its leisure and spa complex.

The Marquess of Londonderry opened up a number of local pits and became very angry with the nearby docks at Sunderland when he accused them of grossly overcharging him for shipping coal out of his collieries. He decided the solution was to build his own harbour at Seaham. It opened in 1831 and took only 3 years to build. The present town grew up around the harbour. By 1851 more than 2,000 vessels were using the new facilities, now complete with lighthouse and navigational aids. However, the harbour became inadequate to deal with the millions of tonnes of coal. Further land was reclaimed and the dock was deepened and extended. It was opened in 1905 and consisted of an unusual series of interconnecting locks.

More pits were opened in the area and finally overloaded the capacity at Seaham Harbour. The answer was to build the Londonderry Railway, six miles long, to Sunderland and intervening stations. The first mineral train used the line in 1855. Inevitably Seaham suffered its disasters as did many mining villages and ports. Two explosions at Seaham Colliery accounted for many lives. The first happened in 1871, killing 26 miners and many ponies stabled 1½ miles away - some blast! Two men, father and son, triggered the blast when shot-firing. The son died but the father, whilst seriously injured, lived on. Just nine years later a second explosion occurred claiming the lives of 164 men and boys. The father who escaped death in the 1871 explosion was killed on this occasion. The mass funerals attracted some 40,000 people to the area.

1870 saw the arrival of the first R.N.L.I. Lifeboat, the "Sisters Carter". In 1872 a dreadful storm at sea occurred. Newspapers reported that six Seaham based ships were sunk with all hands. In 1962 a coble from Seaham, out on a fishing trip, started to take in water due to rough seas. Seaham's lifeboat, "The George Elmy", put out to sea to rescue them. The four were transferred into the lifeboat which then headed back to harbour. As the lifeboat reached the piers it was hit by a series of massive waves and overturned. All of the lifeboat crew drowned and there was only one survivor from the coble.

R.W. Thornton

85

Hartlepool

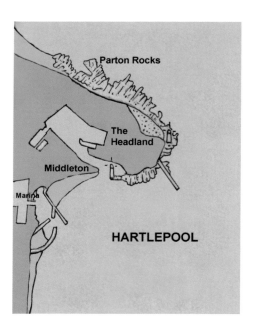

HARTLEPOOL

artlepool is a bustling seaside resort with a wide range of attractions for its increasing number of visitors. It boasts one of the biggest and best marinas in the country, capable of berthing up to 500 vessels. It is now home to a wide variety of pleasure and working craft, with passage to and from the sea aided by a lock.

The Historic Quay regeneration, a fascinating project, was a previous winner in the "Large Visitor Attraction of the Year". The entire quayside boasts an intriguing range of shops and buildings in authentic period style. Here you see chandlers, gunsmiths, swordsmiths, naval tailors and many more 'shops'. Moored nearby is a floating 'museum', the frigate "Trincomalee", launched in 1817 and beautifully restored.

Hartlepool originated as a village in the 7th century, centred around Hartlepool Abbey, founded in 640AD on a headland overlooking a natural harbour. The monastery became famous under St. Hilda, who served as its Abbess from 649AD – 657AD. It fell into decline and was destroyed by the Vikings in 800AD. Hart is the old English name for deer and pool meant by the sea, hence Hartlepool. It was thought that in prehistoric times the headland may have been a tidal island and it and the surrounding shores were covered by thick forests.

During the Middle Ages the village grew into a small, important town, gaining a market and enclosed by a limestone wall. Its harbour was improved to serve as the official port for the Bishops of Durham. The town had medicinal springs which became well known. Thomas Gray commented, "I have been for two days to taste the water, and I do assure you that nothing could be saltier and bitterer and nastier and better for you".

Throughout the Middle Ages, Hartlepool virtually monopolised the shipping trade and was one of the busiest ports on the eastern coast. It was so important that it regularly attracted pirates who hampered trade in the area. However, by the 18th century Hartlepool's importance as a port had fallen into serious decline.

Unbelievably the natural harbour was enclosed for agricultural purposes and corn was grown on the harbour slake. I'll bet the fishermen had a few words to say about that!

In 1813 the enclosure was lifted and the harbour saved. It was now accepted that further trade had to be brought into the town to save it from oblivion. 1835 saw the completion of a railway to allow South Durham coal to be exported. A rival railway was built in 1847, its terminus forming the hub of a new town called West Hartlepool. The two communities increased dramatically - from a population of only 1,000 at the start of the 19th century to 64,000 by 1891. The two towns were formally united in 1967. By 1913 no fewer than forty three ship-owning companies were located in the town with responsibility for 236 ships. This was an incredible turnaround for a port that nearly died. However it brought its problems. It became a key target for German bombers and naval vessels in the First World War. One of the first German offensives was a raid on Hartlepool and neighbouring ports. Hartlepool was hit with a total of 1,150 shells, killing 117 residents, and the first military casualty on British soil since the English Civil War.

R.W. Thornton

Seaton Carew

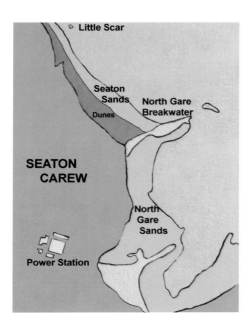

S eaton Carew is a small seaside resort situated between Hartlepool and the mouth of the River Tees. The town derives its name from the French family called Carou who owned a large amount of land in the area. The name Seaton means settlement by the sea – hence Seaton Carew. It was a popular bathing beach for the Darlington Quakers. Its best days were possibly in the 19th century when rows of pretty cottages were built along the seafront. They surrounded The Green, a beautifully lawned square looking onto the sea. Sadly little was added in the way of amenities and Seaton Carew's charm began to fade. However, recent regeneration work has done much to restore the town's vitality and attraction. A promenade now allows visitors to walk from Hartlepool Marina to Seaton Carew, offering wonderful unrestricted views of the North Sea. The town is noted for its firework display and carnival which attracts thousands of visitors from across the region to celebrate Bonfire Night. The local golf course opened in 1874 and is the oldest golf course in County Durham.

The stretch of coast between Hartlepool and Seaton Carew was regarded as one of the most dangerous areas for shipping – leading to countless wrecks. In 1861 lifeboats from Hartlepool and Seaton Carew were called out when one of the worst storms in memory hit the North East Coast. 70 ships came to grief but the lifeboats saved forty lives and escorted a further 91 vessels safely into port. In January 1907 the "SS Clavering" went ashore near the North Gare breakwater with a crew of 39. The Seaton Carew lifeboat managed to rescue 15 crew but further attempts to reach the vessel were abandoned because of the conditions. The Hartlepool lifeboat was brought round by road to assist in the rescue. Both boats made another attempt to reach the "Clavering", but again the attempt had to be abandoned at two o'clock in the morning. In daylight with the weather easing they successfully reached the stranded ship and rescued the remaining 24 crew. In all the operation took nearly 37 hours in atrocious weather. A truly heroic effort.

One wreck, however, did help the people of Seaton Carew in a spectacular way. In 1867 a severe storm pounded the coast and because of the lack of sea defences in those days most of the sand was washed away from the beach, leaving the rocks uncovered.

The story goes that in the early morning two men, cold and fed up, were trudging along the beach on their way to Middlesborough seeking work. They encountered a patch of sea coal and, in kicking it away, one of the men picked a piece up to fling into the sea. There appeared to be something strange about it so he wiped it on his sleeve. It was a gold coin! They started to search and couldn't believe it when they found the beach littered with Spanish doubloons. They stuffed their pockets with coins - then used their overcoats as bags into which they stuffed even more coins and then staggered off home. Their families returned and using various containers, including chamber pots, collected more treasure.

In 1996, two local people when walking along the beach discovered a wreck that had not been seen in at least 50 years. A recent storm had stripped sand off the beach and exposed the wreck. It lay in the mid-tide zone with bows towards the shore and appears to have been a collier brig. A photograph taken in 1898 appears to be that of the same wreck. It may have been subject to salvage in the past, possibly to remove its cargo of coal. At the time of its discovery it soon became apparent that what the sea had revealed, would soon be covered again as each incoming tide brought in more sand to cover the wreck. Its importance was recognised under the Protection of Wrecks legistration.

R.W THORNTON

89

The Tees to the Humber

"I never was on the dull tame shore,
But I loved the great sea more and more;
And backward flew to her billowy breast,
Like a bird that seeketh its mother's nest,
And a mother she was, and is to me,
For I was born on the open sea."

from "The Sea" by Bryan Waller Procter (1787 - 1874)

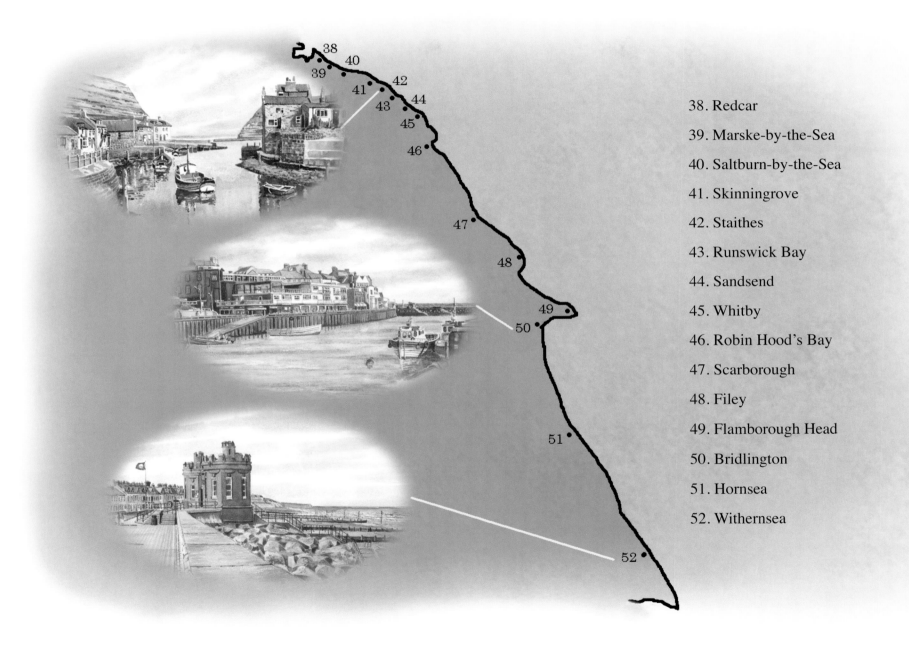

38. Redcar

39. Marske-by-the-Sea

40. Saltburn-by-the-Sea

41. Skinningrove

42. Staithes

43. Runswick Bay

44. Sandsend

45. Whitby

46. Robin Hood's Bay

47. Scarborough

48. Filey

49. Flamborough Head

50. Bridlington

51. Hornsea

52. Withernsea

Redcar

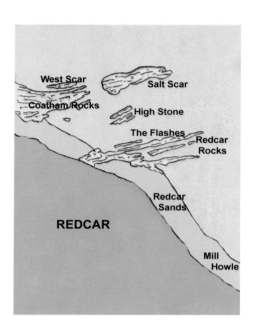

West Scar

Salt Scar

Coatham Rocks

High Stone

The Flashes

Redcar Rocks

Redcar Sands

REDCAR

Mill Howle

Redcar is a seaside resort which lies south of Middlesborough. It was a small fishing town in the early 14th century and supplied the market town of Coatham to the north. In 1846 work was completed on the Middlesborough and Redcar Railway and introduced holiday makers to a beautiful 8 mile stretch of sand going as far as Saltburn-by-the-Sea. From the 1800s to the present day Redcar has had its donkey rides. The donkeys used today are owned by the Burniston family, who have hired donkeys out for over a century.

Also on the seafront is a museum run by the RNLI. Here is the "Zetland", claimed to be the world's oldest lifeboat. She was built in South Shields in 1800 and was originally stationed at Spurn Head before arriving in Redcar in 1802. Throughout her distinguished career of 80 years service she saved more than 502 lives. Also worth a mention is the Grade II listed clockwork tower, a memorial to King Edward V11 who was a regular visitor to Redcar. The cobles still fish from Redcar, mainly for lobster and crabs; they also take holidaymakers out on sea trips. Around 1900 the main North Yorkshire fishing ports were Redcar, Staithes and Whitby, each harbouring some fifty cobles.

Whilst tourism was an important source of income over the year, the discovery of iron ore in the region led to a large increase in population. The town's main employer was Dorman Long Steelworks founded in 1917, and ICI Wilton Chemical works post-war. The steel produced at Dorman Long has an impressive record, being used in the construction of the Sydney Harbour Bridge, Tyne Bridge, Auckland Harbour Bridge and many others. Steel is made by Corus using iron produced by the company's Redcar blast furnace, the largest in Europe.

Whilst Redcar has enjoyed success with tourism and steel production the same cannot be said about its pier construction. Plans for Redcar pier were produced in 1866, but didn't begin until 1871. Meanwhile work began on a pier in nearby Coatham. Misfortune befell both piers. The Coatham pier was wrecked before completion when two sailing ships were driven clean through it as a result of a terrible storm. It was eventually repaired and boasted two kiosks, an entrance with a roller-skating rink and a bandstand. In 1898 a barque named "The Birger" sailed into the pier and virtually wrecked it. Enough being enough, the pier was allowed to disintegrate. Some attempts were made to revive the remains of the pier by the addition of a glass house where concerts were played. This was replaced by the New Pavilion Theatre in 1928 which became the Regent cinema in early 1960s.

Disaster struck the Redcar Pier in the 1880s when the brig "Luna" struck it, causing a great deal of damage. In 1885, "SS Cochrane" destroyed the landing stage. This was on New Year's Eve – so some questions could be asked! In 1897 the schooner "Amarant" went clean through the pier and the following year the pier head burnt down. 1907 saw a pavilion ballroom built and in 1928 the pavilion was extended. Repeated storm damage over the years led to its demolition in 1981.

A recent development which aroused a great deal of interest was the choice of Redcar as the location for filming Ian McEwan's novel "Atonement". The production company searched the country for a town that could still pass as Dunkirk in the 1940s and the only place that was suitable was Redcar. The Coatham Hotel, Regent Cinema, Newcomen Terrace and part of the beach were 'dressed' as 1940 Dunkirk. Railings and lamp posts were replaced with authentic cast iron versions. Tanks were half sunk in the sand and a flotilla of small 60 year old boats lay beyond the breaker.

R.W. THORNTON

93

Marske-by-the-Sea

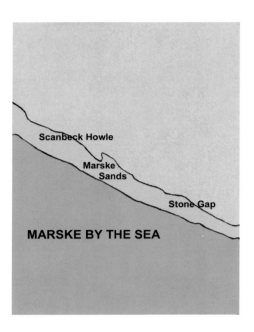

Scanbeck Howle

Marske Sands

Stone Gap

MARSKE BY THE SEA

Marske-by-the-Sea is the first village south of Redcar on the coast. It is here that brightly painted cobles can still be found lining the shore below the old cottages in the narrow street sloping down to the beach. Whilst fishing still takes place, the majority of Marske residents are employed in nearby industry. Marske, or "Mersc", meaning marshland as it was called, did not escape the brutal wars that raged the country. In 657AD Hilda, a nun, settled in the area near to where Spoutbeck joins the sea, close to a source of fresh water and sea coal. The Vikings arrived in 857AD and two years of feuding and bloodshed followed. In the 11th century William the Conqueror came up north to the Marske marshes and squashed the uprising instigated by Edgar the Atheling.

William Pennyman bought the Manor of Marske and in 1625 he built on the site the imposing mansion of Marske Hall. In 1643 James Pennyman became Lord of the Manor. He was a Royalist and during the Civil War he recruited an army from among his tenants and led them into battle against Oliver Cromwell on Marske beach in the same year. This was not looked upon favourably and he was fined £1,200 – a considerable sum in those days. This may have strengthened his decision to sell the estate in 1650. In 1762 the Dundas family acquired the estate and it became home to the Marquess of Zetland. Charles Dickens visited the town to view Marske Hall's strikingly unusual turrets and to see the graves of Captain Cook's parents. In 1961 Lord Zetland donated the Hall to the Leonard Cheshire Foundation.

Another interesting building, but not as grand as Marske Hall, is "Winkies Castle". It is by no means a castle but is an old cruck house and was owned by the late cobbler, Jack Anderson. It is the oldest remaining building in Marske and is now a folk museum containing over 6,000 artefacts. Jack never lived there but stored equipment from his cobblers business on the premises. The sole inhabitant was Winkie the cat. Mr. Anderson, who died in 2001, left the building and the artefacts he had collected over many years to the people of Marske.

Another old manor in Marske is Cliff House which stands on the cliff tops overlooking the beach – see main painting. This was built in the 19th century as a holiday residence for the Pease family who lived in Durham. They were prominent in local business and supported the people of Marske in many ways.

Charlotte Marion Hughes is the longest lived person ever recorded in the United Kingdom at 115 years 228 days. For her 110th birthday she flew on "Concorde" to New York, staying there for four days. Charlotte lived in her own house in Marske until she was 108 years old. She then moved to a nursing home in Redcar and remained mentally alert to the end of her life.

R.W. THORNTON

Saltburn-by-the-Sea

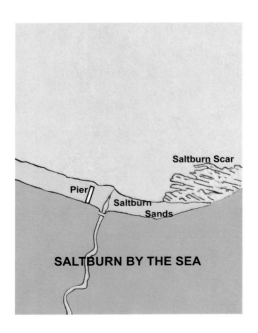

The Pease family, who had a holiday home on the cliff tops in nearby Marske-by-the-Sea, played a huge part in the development of Saltburn. Before 1860 Saltburn was a tiny fishing village lying below the steep cliffs next to the "Ship Inn". The story goes that Henry Pease was staying with his brother in Marske and returned rather late for dinner. The reason he gave was that he had walked to Saltburn and while sitting on the cliffs overlooking the beach he had a 'vision'. He saw below a seaside resort that would outdo any along the coast. It included the Zetland Hotel, Pier, Cliff Lift, The Valley Gardens and the so-called 'jewel streets'. These streets were named Ruby, Emerald, Garnet, Pearl and Diamond. George Dickinson of Darlington was asked to draw up a plan of the town. Within 20 years the basic form of the town was constructed. The Zetland Hotel was reputed to be the world's first purpose built Railway Hotel with its own private platform. The project was completed when the Cliff Lift was built in 1870.

The resort was unashamedly designed for middle class Victorian visitors - in the early years 'excursion' trains were not allowed to stop here. It became an immediate success. To transport visitors from the elegant town on the cliff tops down 150ft. to the promenade and pier below an ingenious water-balanced Tramway was constructed. It is still in use and is the oldest such Tramway to survive in Britain. Two cars run on parallel lines and each has a tank underneath. The car at the top has its tank filled with water until it overbalances the weight of the bottom car and then gravity takes over and the top car descends at the same time as the bottom car ascends. The Cliff Lift carries over 70,000 passengers each year.

Saltburn's iron pier was the first of its kind to be built on the North East coast. Completed in 1869, it consisted of iron trestles under a wooden deck. The pier was 1,400ft. long. Within ten years of opening a number of fierce gales destroyed the pier head, the landing stage, and parts of the pier deck. When the damage was repaired the length of the pier was reduced to 1,250ft. Throughout the years it suffered disaster after disaster – the cost of repairs became unaffordable and in 1975 the council applied to have the pier demolished. A compromise was reached that only the last 13 trestles should be removed and the remainder of the pier restored. It was officially reopened in 2001.

Smuggling was considered an accepted way of life to help combat the heavy taxes imposed by the government. Extreme violence could be carried out by smugglers towards those who attempted to interfere with their trade in contraband. Legend has it that Saltburn conceals a maze of secret smugglers' passages.

Saltburn's most famous smuggler was John Andrew. He was born in Scotland and moved to Saltburn in 1870 after marrying the niece of Will Harrison, landlord of the "Ship Inn" on the beachfront. He soon became the landlord and a respected member of the Saltburn community, so much so that he was often called on by the local customs officers to help them track down the smugglers. Rather ironic when he was one of their main targets. Part of the Saltburn smugglers code were the words whispered around the community, "Andrew's cow has calved". It informed the inhabitants that the smugglers boat was offshore and ready to be unloaded. Apparently one of the main routes to smuggle the goods once they were ashore was via the "Ship Inn" through a secret passage up the cliffs to the "White House". John Andrew was eventually captured in 1827 but his loot has never been discovered.

R.W. THORNTON

Skinningrove

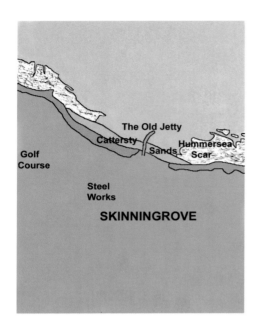

The Old Jetty
Cattersty
Hummersea
Sands
Scar
Golf
Course
Steel
Works
SKINNINGROVE

Skinningrove is a village that nestles in a secluded valley between the two highest cliffs on Britain's coastline, Hummersea and Boulby Cliffs to the east and Cattersty Cliff to the west. Skinningrove was once a centre for fishing and smuggling.

Whilst fishing for many years was the main trade the early 1800s saw a new venture. Ironstone nodules eroded from the cliff faces and were scattered about the foreshore. These were loaded by hand into small boats beached between the tides and then shipped to Tyneside's blast furnaces. In 1865 the extension of the railway network to Skinningrove opened much wider ironstone markets. In 1874 the first local blast furnaces were opened, leading to the construction of a substantial jetty in the harbour below the cliffs in order to allow larger ships to handle much heavier cargoes. The jetty was built in 1886 by the Skinningrove Iron Company. Concrete was thought not to be strong enough so it was constructed of a unique mixture, at that time, of molten slag washed in cold water, crushed and then mixed with cement. It was anticipated that this would increase durability. A railway track ran from the mine down an incline and along the length of the jetty.

Before men started digging into the bowels of the earth this was a fishing village. It is recorded that in the year 1553, the fishermen of Skinningrove hauled up a 'sea-man' in their nets. Ancient documents do not afford much detail. We are not even told if he had a fish-tail as you would expect of a 'mer-man'. The men of the village kept him in a disused house for several weeks and fed him on raw fish. Many visitors came to see him but could not communicate as he only squeaked, however he seemed to be personable and enjoying the attention. The novelties of shore life evidently palled and he escaped to the beach. As he made his way out to sea he repeatedly smiled and waved and then with one final salute he vanished beneath the waves never to be seen again. Like me you will find this a tall story, but it is documented and well known. Did some sort of incident occur that was so unusual? Unfortunately we'll never know.

The face of Skinningrove was changed forever by the discovery of ironstone. The population of just 63 in 1841 swelled to 1,700 in 1881. Extensive building work took place and from a quiet village it was transformed into an industrial township - from a mere 13 buildings to 348 in just 10 years. Many of these were tightly packed brick cottages laid out in grid form. Thankfully the terraced cottages at the harbour entrance have maintained their picturesque appearance. These, along with the allotments, pigeon lofts and maze of fishermens' huts, remind us of what a close linked community Skinningrove was.

At the moment the public are barred from the jetty in the harbour because of health and safety regulations. As can be expected anglers still risk life and limb in pursuing their pastime. Local councillors are pushing hard for the jetty's restoration. They claim that it is a site of historic importance and it would also provide docking facilities for sea trips as well as help the coastline which is eroding rapidly. Let us hope their efforts are rewarded.

R.W. THORNTON

Staithes

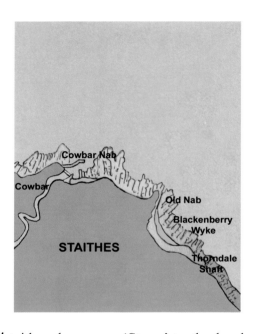

Staithes, known as 'Steers' to the locals, was once one of the largest fishing ports on the North East coast, with a fishing fleet of 120 boats employing some 300 men. It was also an important source of minerals. Near the highest cliffs in England, this beautiful grouping of stone houses with red pan-tiled roofs huddled around the harbour make it one of the most attractive spots on the coastal stretch. The steep outcrop of Cowbar Nab – nab meaning promontory – far more romantic and much easier to pronounce – protects the northern flank of the village from the sea. Storms and floods have plagued Staithes over the centuries. The famous pub "The Cod and Lobster" situated down in the harbour has been rebuilt 3 times. I have enjoyed many hours sitting in the harbour overwhelmed by the choice of subjects to paint.

To reach Staithes you pass through modern housing on the cliff top which does not prepare you for what is to come. Staithes itself is relatively untouched by modern times, consisting of interesting alleyways including Dog Loup, the narrowest street in Northern England. These are well worth exploring before you come to the harbour.

Staithes has attracted artists for many years. The famous Staithes Group was formed in the late 19th century by Dame Ethel Walker RA and many came to reside in Staithes. They numbered around 30 and set a high standard in Impressionist painting, often using the fishing families as models at three pence a session. If the artists were caught painting on a Sunday they were pelted with fish heads! Their work is now represented in major public collections and in the Tate Gallery.

Staithes' best known character is James Cook. He came to Staithes in 1744 as a sixteen-year old apprentice to William Sanderson, a local grocer and draper. James soon tired of the boredom of shopkeeping and being so close to the sea and bustling boats he quickly developed an interest in all things maritime. Mr. Sanderson apparently helped him to move on to Whitby where a ship owner employed him as a servant on one of his ships. The rest of course is history. It turned out to be a wise move as shortly after, the shop in which he had worked at Staithes fell into the sea after a storm.

The Staithes Heritage Centre and Captain Cook Museum are well worth a visit - the past lives of the fisherfolk are well demonstrated. Of particular interest are the traditional Staithes bonnets, which the fisherwomen used to wear to protect their heads, neck and hair. The bonnets were padded on the top to allow the women to balance the fish baskets on their heads. A flap at the back protected them against run-off water. It is said that Staithes women were noted for their graceful bearing as they had to hold themselves extremely upright to balance the heavy baskets of fish while walking.

Staithes also has its legends. Apparently two mermaids dared to come ashore. The villagers tied them up on the beach while they wondered what to do with them. Whilst they were pondering the tide came in and the mermaids made their escape. As they made their exit they laid a curse on the village that; "the sea shall flow to Jackdaw's Well". The curse came true and shortly after the well was washed from the cliff top - a tall tale or should that be two!

R.W. THORNTON

Runswick Bay

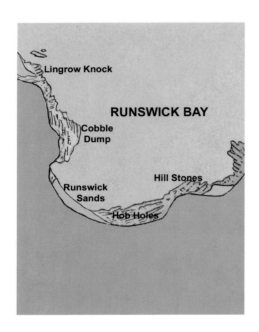

Runswick Bay was inhabited long before Roman times, as burial mounds found on the moors behind have proved. In the 17th and 18th centuries the village depended on fishing and whaling as a way of life, and of course smuggling. Today Runswick Bay is an extremely picturesque seaside village offering a more peaceful ambience for the many visitors who flock there during the summer months. It is also a favourite haunt for artists. The village is virtually two-tiered. A number of houses sited on the cliff tops contrast sharply with the red-roofed cottages that appear to hug the cliffs as they descend to the seafront below. It has proved to be both picturesque and perilous.

In 1682 a great storm washed away sections of the cliff causing a landslide that destroyed the whole village with the exception of just one house - unbelievably no one was injured. Two mourners attending a wake realised what was happening and ran to warn the inhabitants and the village was quickly evacuated. Their action no doubt saved many lives; there would have been few survivors. The village was rebuilt with the help of a Disaster Fund. Its precarious position was highlighted yet again when another storm-induced landslide destroyed a small iron-smelting works and cracks were appearing in the walls of the cottages as recently as 1969. The decision to build a significant sea wall to offer protection was welcomed and the defensive wall was completed in 1970.

In nearby cliffs there is a system of caves known as the "Hob Holes" where the "Hob Goblin" is reputed to live. The goblin is supposed to have held the cure for whooping cough – a deadly illness at the time. Local mothers would bring their ailing 'bairns' to the mouth of the cave and shout down to the goblin, begging for their children to be cured. The success rate is not known!

Runswick had its own lifeboat with quite a history - Kettleness Point on the far side of the bay has been the scene of many shipwrecks. In 1901 the lifeboat was launched and manned entirely by the women of the village as their men were trapped out at sea in their fishing boats. Despite the appalling conditions all the men were saved. The old thatched coastguard's cottage, lifeboat house and boat park still stand at the edge of the village. The lifeboat sadly moved to Staithes in 1978 but a rescue service still operates.

As well as fishing, local alum deposits were here from the early 17th century and the ruins of the old workings are still visible. At one time there was also jet mining. The use of jet in jewellery declined at the end of Queen Victoria's reign. It can still be picked up along the shore.

Like many fishing ports Runswick Bay has its fair share of strange superstitions. The Reverend Cooper of Filey was appalled when he discovered one that led to death by drowning. He learned that the locals believed it was unlucky to save a drowning man. The Vicar discovered that men being dragged ashore were abandoned on the advice of the village elders, "lest ill-fortune should result from saving them".

The steep cliffs and sandy bay created a natural shelter for boats to be pulled in safely after a fishing trip. There are few fulltime fishermen left but there are still fishing related links. Leisure fishing is very popular from the bay, often at night.

R.W. THORNTON

Sandsend

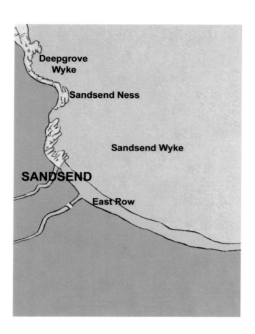

From Runswick Bay the road drops down the steep Lythe Bank to Sandsend. An extremely attractive village, it lies at the mouth of the Mulgrave Beck which runs for 3 miles through the dense and beautiful Mulgrave Woods down to the shore. It is rare to see such a dense cluster of trees so near the sea on the east coast; they add a most welcome touch of 'softness' to the resort. At Sandsend the striking cliffs of North Yorkshire disappear for a while, to be replaced by 2½ miles of glorious sand leading all the way to Whitby. From this point the majestic ruins of the Abbey appear in all their glory.

In the past Sandsend was a Victorian fishing port but peaceful as it seems now, it did not escape the ongoing sieges and battles that raged for centuries. This is indicated by the faint remains of Lythe Castle which contained an earthwork motte and bailey fort and the more substantial relics of Mulgrave Castle.

Legend has it that this early castle was built for 'Wada the Giant' a 6th century chief. A solid castle was built in the 13th century by the Fossard Family, who were given the land after the Norman Conquest. It was defended by the Royalists during the Civil War and so suffered the usual fate of such buildings after the Parliamentary victory. The castle was demolished, with the help of cannons, in 1647. A mansion was built for Lady Catherine Darnley, the illegitimate daughter of King James II in the late 17th century.

The estate now belongs to Lord Normanby. Two well-known visitors in the past were Charles Dickens and William Wordsworth. An even more colourful character to stay was an Indian Maharajah – Duleep Singh. He rented the castle in 1859 while the Marquis of Normanby was abroad and lived there for 5 years complete with elephants which he had brought over from India. He would go shooting on the moors while dressed in full Indian regalia, accompanied by attendants in similar colourful attire. There is no mention of the elephants accompanying them!

In 1939, a German Heinkel bomber was chased by Spitfires some 20 miles off Whitby. It was shot down. Two days later the two survivors of the four-man crew landed in a rubber dinghy near Sandsend - they were the first Germans of the Second World War to be captured on English soil. Both men were extremely exhausted, one was barely conscious so their 'capture' was more of a 'rescue'. The airmen remained so grateful to their rescuers that they arranged to meet up again in 1979 – a truly heart-warming story.

Sandsend Ness is an old alum-quarrying site which offered near ideal conditions for the rapidly expanding alum industry from the early 17th century onwards. The process was of such a scale and duration that significant parts of the Yorkshire coast were permanently changed. Alum was used extensively in the leather and dye industry. Another industry from the past was cement making. Remains of the kilns can be seen where the 'Roman' cement was made. This was made from locally collected stone and had the great advantage that it would set under water – a huge asset for building sea walls and harbour quays.

One of the delights of Sandsend is the availability of fossils. The group of fossils named ammonites has an interesting history. One of the ammonites is named Hildoceras after the Abbess of Whitby, St. Hilda. It was believed that these were snakes that were beheaded and turned into stone by St. Hilda.

R.W. THORNTON

105

Whitby

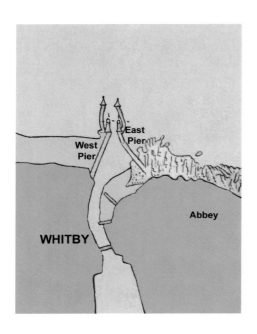

Whitby is one of Yorkshire's most historic and attractive towns. It lies beyond Kettleness where the red roofs huddle along both banks of the River Esk, dividing the town into two distinctive halves joined by the swing bridge. To the south of the Esk there are picturesque narrow streets and interesting alleyways fronted by intriguing shops and a delightful harbour, all overlooked from above by the stately ruins of Whitby Abbey. To the north of the Esk there is a fish market and small harbour where fishing boats lie. Above is West Cliff with its wide streets, elegant crescents, boarding houses and hotels laid out on the cliff tops across the harbour from the old town. Here there is a bronze statue of Captain Cook and the well admired arch formed from the jawbone of a whale.

The establishment of the Abbey at Whitby was due to the Northumbrian King Oswy in 657AD. St.Hilda,

then abbess at Hartlepool, moved in to become the first abbess of Whitby. Years later the Danes raided Northumbria and Whitby Abbey was reduced to ruins. It was these same Danes who gave Whitby its present name Hvitbyr – the white village.

In the 18th century Whitby was a port of significant importance with whaling boats berthed there. The first ships sailed for Greenland in 1753 but it took a number of years before whaling became a viable trade. Initially a ship returning with four or five whales was thought to have had a good catch. This gradually increased to an average of not less than fifteen, yielding 127 tonnes of oil for each ship. In the space of 80 years some 2,761 whales were landed. Much of that success was due to the skills of one of the great whaling captains, William Scaresby and his son, also called William. The elder was celebrated for his great daring and navigational skills. He was also credited with inventing the crows nest thus saving many lives.

Another celebrity was James Cook, Whitby's adopted son and famous navigator who circled the world twice on epic voyages of discovery. He started his illustrious career by sailing colliers out of Whitby Harbour. When the port was at its busiest, the loss of fishermen out at sea was considerable, second only to mining. When a woman was widowed she

was allowed to wear black throughout the year with a pink silk scarf. Thus when she was going about her business, doors were held open for her or she was shepherded to the front of any queue as a mark of respect.

Whitby was the inspiration and setting for Bram Stoker's novel, Dracula, while he was on holiday in Scarborough. This is where Count Dracula, in the form of a wolf, loped ashore from a crewless ship which had drifted ashore beneath the cliffs on which the Abbey stands. Many parts of Whitby are readily identified in the novel and this has sparked keen interest in the Goth fraternity who visit the town twice a year to enjoy a "Vampire Ball".

Frank Meadows Sutcliffe, born in Whitby in 1853, became a famous photographer whose wonderful sepia photographs captured perfectly the atmosphere of the locality in the late Victorian era.

After the death of Prince Albert, jewellery made of Whitby jet (fossilised wood) was the only ornamentation that Queen Victoria would allow herself to wear. People followed her example and as a result Whitby prospered greatly. Visitors can still see jet craftsmen at work in the original Victorian jet works.

R.W. THORNTON

107

Robin Hood's Bay

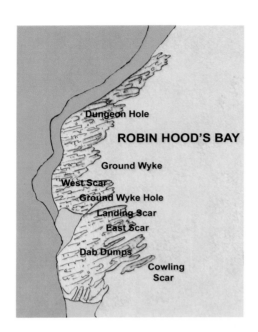

Dungeon Hole

ROBIN HOOD'S BAY

Ground Wyke

West Scar

Ground Wyke Hole

Landing Scar

East Scar

Dab Dumps

Cowling Scar

Six miles south of Whitby lies Robin Hood's Bay, known to the locals as 'Bay'. It is a cluster of red pantiled houses lining a maze of interesting streets and alleyways. The main street drops dramatically down towards the shore. Artists never tire of painting here.

At the bottom of the main street is the "Bay Hotel", its outer walls are washed by the sea at high tide. However, this is not as romantic as it sounds. The previous inn, on the same site, was washed into the sea by a storm in 1843; I only hope 'time' had been called. As elsewhere, coastal erosion is a problem in the 'Bay'. In the 1780s, King Street and 22 cottages fell into the sea after a cliff fall. As late as 1950 Regent Cottage suffered the same fate. Now a coastal defence scheme has provided the village with a concrete facing and retaining wall to stabilise the cliff face and preserve this attractive resort hopefully for many years to come.

The first reference to Robin Hood's Bay comes in 1538 when it was recorded as "a fisher townlet of twenty boats". At that time the settlement consisted of only fifty houses but from that day the activities of the people have been shaped by the sea. It was a thriving fishing port throughout the 18th and 19th centuries but by 1920 there were only two fishing families left. Today occasional small boats fish the harbour and local seas for crab and lobster. Most visitors are extremely curious about how the name Robin Hood came about. Has it any connection with the Robin Hood? There are so many conflicting legends as to how this came about - one that appeals to me is that as Robin Hood and his men came under ever-increasing threat from the Sheriff of Nottingham he arranged for a number of boats to be moored here so he could make a subsequent get-away to sea if the need arose.

Life was not always as relaxed and pleasant as it is today. As well as conflict with the sea the residents faced problems with the Press Gangs who were feared and hated. Fishermen were supposed to be exempt, but their sailing skills often proved their undoing - once 'pressed' their chances of returning home were poor. The village women would beat a drum to warn their menfolk to stay out at sea when the pressmen arrived. Further problems arose with the excise men, hated nearly as much as the Press Gangs. In the 18th century, Robin Hood's Bay was described as the busiest smuggling community on the Yorkshire coast. Its isolation, protected by marshes on all three sides, made it an ideal spot. Fishermen, farmers, clergy and gentry alike were all involved. Fierce battles raged between the two sides; the wives were known to pour boiling water over the excise men from bedroom windows and no doubt other unmentionables! Another source of trouble occurred in the late 1800s. During this period, gangs of labourers were employed on the coastal railway between Whitby and Scarborough - they apparently were hard-drinking, rough-living men who were ever ready for a fight. As well as fighting amongst themselves they often picked on the local residents with sometimes serious injuries caused. There was no prison at the time in the town so those involved had to be taken to Whitby – no easy task. It was decided to build a prison, completed in 1886 at the considerable sum of £1,500. It certainly was not a case of money well spent - apparently a local fisherman and just two labourers spent the night there. There were no further residents!

R.W. THORNTON

Scarborough

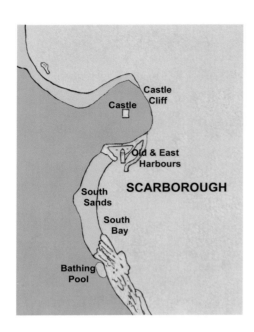

SCARBOROUGH

Castle · Castle Cliff · Old & East Harbours · South Sands · South Bay · Bathing Pool

Scarborough's strategic headland was occupied by man many centuries ago. The remains of a Roman lookout lie on the eastern edge of Castle Cliff. At that time Saxons from Germany were raiding eastern England. If a fleet was sighted signal torches were lit to warn the Roman armed forces. Apparently the town owes its name to a Viking called Thorgil. He had a hare-lip and was given the name 'Skarthi' (meaning hare-lip) so his stronghold became Skarthi'sburgh –Scarborough. The castle which has dominated the town for over 800 years stands on the magnificent headland separating the two bays. The Normans built the large keep, the barbican and the curtain wall which can still be seen today. Although besieged many times it was never taken by assault. Its only surrender came during the Civil War when the garrison was starved of food.

Scarborough, Britain's first seaside resort, has been welcoming visitors for over 360 years. Early 17th century visitors were attracted to its newly discovered mineral springs. At that time a local resident, Mrs. Tomizyn Farrer, was reputed to have discovered a stream of brown acidic water spilling across the shore of South Bay and decided it must possess medicinal properties. The news soon spread and people arrived from far and wide to sample it. I don't know which I admire most, her scientific acumen or her business acumen! The more adventurous spa visitors moved on to the local sands and ventured forth to dip themselves in the bracing sea thus making popular the racy business of sea bathing – a new activity at that time.

With its two splendid sandy bays and dramatic cliff top castle, Scarborough was targeted by early railway tycoons as a natural candidate for Yorkshire's first seaside resort. The railway was completed in 1846 and was followed by the construction of luxury hotels, one of which is the widely admired "Grand Hotel". This building consists of six million bricks and 52 chimneys and today still dominates the cliff tops. As well as hotels, elegant promenades and spacious gardens, there was a fishing and ship building harbour. This splendid layout confirmed the town's claim to the title 'Queen' of watering places. Anne Bronte came here hoping that the Spa's invigorating air would improve her health. Unfortunately it did not and she died at the age of 29. Her grave lies in St.Mary's churchyard at the foot of the castle. The influx of well off visitors caused some trouble in the town at the time. The fishing trade suffered somewhat as the local entrepreneurs claimed that the smell of fish upset the lucrative visitors and could result in a loss of income. Despite this, Scarborough managed to retain a sizeable fishing fleet.

Scarborough is divided into two distinct bays by the coast headland. Each has its own character. The North Bay is a vibrant, fun place echoing most peoples' conception of a seaside resort with its holiday chalets, amusement arcades, parks and miniature railway. The South Bay is a little more sedate with the Spa, Grand Hotel, harbour, clean sands with safe bathing, the Valley Gardens and hydraulic lift giving visitors easy access to the town.

Two traditions handed down over the ages still take place on Shrove Tuesday. Residents have the right to skip along the highways – these days a highly dangerous pastime. This activity is now confined to a small street area. At the same time of the year the locals sound the "Pancake Bell", a custom that began when the women were about to start cooking their pancakes at the beginning of Lent - this was to summon the menfolk from the harbour.

.

R.W. THORNTON

111

Filey

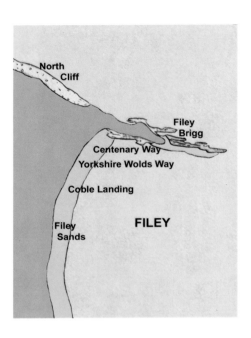

Filey prides itself on its reputation as an ideal family seaside resort and also on being a little more select and quieter than its neighbours – who shall be nameless! Inevitably modern times have brought the usual scattering of amusement arcades, ice cream vendors, fast food outlets etc. But Filey has suffered less than most seaside resorts with its many public parks, gardens and attractive wooded ravine sloping down to the coble landing, all of this topped off by the crescent of elegant white hotels above the promenade. To the north of the town lies Filey Brigg, a massive mile long breakwater protecting the town from winter storms. The name Brigg comes from the Norse, meaning jetty or landing place. It has the remains of a Roman lookout and throughout the years was a graveyard for countless vessels. At very low tide a range of rocks known as the Spittals, halfway along to the Brigg can be seen stretching out to the sea like a finger pointing south east.

The population of Filey in 1801 was 505. The real expansion began when a certain Mr. Unett laid out plans and then began to develop Filey. He bought 7 acres of land and built the Crescent, later known as the Royal Crescent. It was opened in the 1840s and for a hundred years it was the most fashionable address in the North of England. This with the opening of the railway in 1846 made Filey a rapidly growing holiday resort that attracted many of the gentry. Filey has an impressive list of holidaymakers. These include Jenny Lind *The Swedish Nightingale*, Charlotte Bronte, Frederic Delius the composer and Dame Myra Hess, the pianist.

Canon A.N. Cooper claimed that it was the coming of the Primitive Methodists to Filey in 1823 "that well-nigh turned the place upside down, and from superstition, ignorance and wickedness, the inhabitants became sober, intelligent and God fearing people". To some extent this is supported by the following extract from an early guide to bathing - "nor shall place in the water any bathing machine, containing a male or males, nearer than 130 yards from any other bathing machine containing a female or females". This may not have pleased the residents of Butlins Holiday Camp which was built in Filey in 1939. During the war the camp became a military base. By 1945 it reverted to an extremely popular holiday resort complete with its own railway station, bringing untold prosperity to the town. By the late 1950s the station could cater for 10,000 holidaymakers - it closed in 1984.

My favourite place is the Coble Landing, a cobbled structure at the north end of the beach - it has an interesting mixture of cobles, passenger vessels, pleasure craft, arcades and cafes. The place bustles with activity and it is quite a sight to see the cobles pulled from the sea by tractor and then 'parked' on the Landing and the promenade. Altogether there are 7 traditional fishing cobles and 24 leisure craft. As elsewhere the fishing port has declined, records show that as early as the 12th century Filey men were fishing as far away as Whitby and Grimsby. The sands were used in 1910 for the Blackburn flying school and it was here that the first fatal aviation crash involving a passenger took place: both pilot and passenger died.

In 1974 the boundary between the East and North Ridings was changed. This cut through Filey and left the town lying in East Riding and the churchyard in the North Riding. This peculiar arrangement fed the wry Yorkshire humour. When they learnt of someone's illness they came out with, "Aye, he'll soon be in the North Riding" – the graveyard!

R.W. THORNTON

Flamborough Head

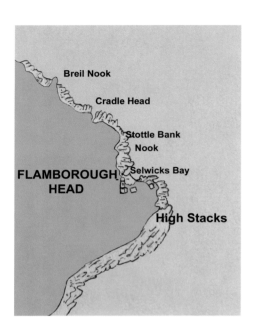

A t Flamborough Head the sea and land are locked in ceaseless battle. The 400 ft. high chalk cliffs boast coves, sea caves and stacks, all carved out by the relentless pounding of waves. Paradoxically this 'wanton' destruction has produced one of the most picturesque stretches on the Yorkshire coast – much visited and much photographed. The cliffs are home to one of the largest sites of nesting sea birds in England. The name Flamborough has uncertain origins. It is thought to be derived from a word meaning "the place of the flame". Other sources claim it comes from the Saxon word "Flaen" meaning dart, which the headland shape resembles.

The village of Flamborough lies a little way inland from the coast. It has a 12th century church and the remains of a 14th century castle. The North Landing is one of two coves used by local fishermen - the other being the South Landing on the far side of the headland. The people of Flamborough apparently did not take readily to outsiders and were extremely superstitious. No boat would sail on a Sunday, wool could only be wound during daylight and the mention of a hare or pig meant that they would not sail on that tide. No fisherman would dare leave the harbour unless he was wearing the navy-blue jersey knitted by his wife with a pattern exclusive to the village. Many such superstitions appear to be shared along the North East coast.

Between the two landings the massive headland is dart shaped. On the very tip stands a plain square whitewashed building which houses the bellowing foghorn – sleepless nights for some no doubt! Further inland rises the 92 ft tower of the lighthouse – arguably one of the most photographed in the country. It is open to visitors where you can see the spinning lantern cradle floating on a base of mercury. The lighthouse was built in 1806 and cost £8,000 - it signalled 4 white flashes. Further developments included a foghorn and radio signals. It was the last manned on the East Coast until it became automated in 1995.

The remains of Flamborough Head's first lighthouse still stands a little way inland from the present one. An octagonal chalk tower built in 1674, it is England's oldest surviving lighthouse. The beacon was a basket of coal. Apparently it was built by John Mason, a Bridlington builder, the job being completed in just 9 months!

Access to Flamborough Head can be gained via Bempton Cliffs, punctuated by narrow coves with sheer drops of 400 feet into the sea – a dangerous place to be! These cliffs were happy hunting grounds for the Bempton climbers until fairly recently. Known as the "climmers", these were local men who, in the summer, were lowered over the edges of these precipitous cliffs by rope to collect gulls' eggs. This was stopped in 1955 by the Wild Birds Protection Act.

Flamborough Head witnessed one of the most stubborn naval battles in British history during the American War of Independence. Locals on the Head gazed transfixed as battle commenced out at sea. In 1779 an American/Continental Navy Squadron led by John Paul Jones faced up to two British escort vessels protecting a large merchant convoy. Battle commenced and the English escort vessels were captured by the notorious Jones who also fired on the quiet little town of Alnmouth.

R.W. THORNTON

115

Bridlington

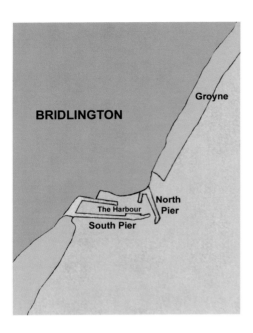

The ancient market town, once known as Birlington, lies about a mile inland from the coast. This has been overtaken by Bridlington Quay, which is the home of the tourist area and the harbour which lies just south of Flamborough Head. Ten miles of sandy beach, award winning promenades and historic harbour this is one of the country's best-loved seaside resorts. Here there is a mixture of traditional entertainment, funfair, amusement arcades, donkey rides and more modern attractions such as Leisure World. These are balanced by ornamental gardens, parks, pleasant promenades and Sewerby Hall. This is an outstanding Georgian mansion connected to the town by both footpath and miniature railway. Situated in a dramatic cliff top position, the Hall was built between 1714–1720. It is surrounded by 50 acres of garden and parkland and was first opened to the public in 1936 by Amy Johnson, the romantic Yorkshire born pilot who thrilled the world with her daring solo flights to South Africa and Australia. Here there are now formal gardens, park, museum, art gallery, bowls and a zoo.

The focal point for visitors is undoubtedly the harbour. Bridlington grew up around the harbour, which has been here since the Middle Ages, and once enjoyed a steady trade in livestock and coal. For many years it was an important fishing port. This has declined dramatically over the years although there are still some fishing boats left. Today the harbour hosts mainly yachts and pleasure craft. Trips out to Flamborough Head are very popular. An R.A.F. air-sea rescue base has been stationed here since the 1930s. T.E. Lawrence (Lawrence of Arabia) was stationed here as an aircraftsman.

Bridlington's first hotel opened in the early 19th century and the town developed very quickly. The elegant houses along the seafront were built mainly by wealthy Yorkshire families. They were greatly upset in 1842 by the arrival of the railways which brought in common day-trippers and hordes of holidaymakers from the nearby mills and steel towns. Donkey rides were introduced and the Bridlington Spa and Gardens were opened in 1896. Today the resort caters for all kinds of visitors. Regretably Bridlington's popularity has declined along with other resorts.

Bridlington's first lifeboat was established in 1806. One of the worst shipping disasters along this stretch of the coast happened in 1871 in Bridlington Bay. During a memorable storm 46 sailors perished and the lifeboat crew, on their way to save lives, were thrown into the water a few yards from the pier and most of the crew perished. This dreadful tragedy is still recalled each year with a solemn service of remembrance when the lifeboat is drawn through the town.

It was here in 1643 that Queen Henrietta Maria landed from a Dutch ship that was laden with arms and aid for her beleaguered husband, Charles I. Parliamentary naval vessels were in hot pursuit and having failed to catch their quarry bombarded the town. Apparently cannon balls actually struck the building where she was lodging, forcing her to take refuge in a ditch. What price dignity!

R.W. THORNTON

117

Hornsea

Hornsea boasts a golden, sandy beach with a newly developed promenade a mile in length and incorporating a series of 'groyne gardens' adding to the beach theme. The improved access, increased seating areas and the sensitive positioning of lawns and plants have made a most attractive addition to this seaside resort. The promenade has recently been resurfaced and further development includes cafes and beach huts.

At the beginning of the 19th century, Hornsea had a population of just 533 and the settlement was primarily agricultural in character. The increasing popularity of sea bathing from the end of the 18th century led to the development of Hornsea as a 'watering place'. This attracted mainly middle class visitors. Throughout these writings I have been struck by the fact that sea bathing down this stretch of the coast was undertaken by the Victorian middle class. The explanation is obvious: they and they only had the transport to reach

the coast. Once again it was the opening of the railway line that transformed Hornsea. This worked in two ways. People could now move to Hornsea to live by the sea and commute to jobs inland. 'Trippers' from inland could now visit the coast at a reasonable cost. Charlotte Bronte stayed in Hornsea for several weeks to 'take the waters'. Apparently the highlight of the season in those days was the horse racing which took place along the beach for two weeks every year.

Victorian seaside resorts were expected to have a pier and Hornsea was no exception. After many arguments, problems and setbacks the pier was completed in 1880, only to be damaged by a ship blown into it during a storm. The remains of the pier were repaired but it was 250 yards shorter than the original. It was opened in 1881 but became a financial liability and was sold for scrap a few years later. The early part of the 20th century saw several schemes designed to attract holidaymakers. The sea wall and promenade were extended to give protection from flooding; this included a restaurant and amusement arcade. However, traders and showmen were deterred from setting up in Hornsea due to the local Council. They insisted that amusements and fish and chip vendors were not allowed to open on a Sunday. This at a time when most working class people only had a Sunday

off, and so tended to go off on day trips to seaside resorts for a lively day out. An unbelievable situation until you learn that the Council in question were influenced in their decisions by a residential lobby that was opposed, or even hostile to visitors and wanted Hornsea as quiet residential place to live.

Hornsea Mere is the largest natural lake in Yorkshire. It was created by glacial action and is 2 miles long and a mile wide and lies ½ mile inland. There are over 170 species of birds on site, ideal for birdwatchers who are well catered for. In addition there are facilities for fishing, boating and sailing.

During the Middle Ages there were a number of disputes between St. Mary's Abbey in York and Meaux Abbey near Beverley as to who had the right to take fish from the Mere. At one point the monks resorted by trial to combat. They did not fight themselves but hired thugs to represent them. To some extent the fall in numbers to visit the seaside was compensated by the increasing interest in the growth of Hornsea Pottery. It started as a cottage industry in 1949 and rapidly achieved a worldwide reputation for creative design and manufacturing processes. In the 1990s it found it increasingly difficult to survive due to cheaper imports and the factory closed in 2000.

R.W. THORNTON

119

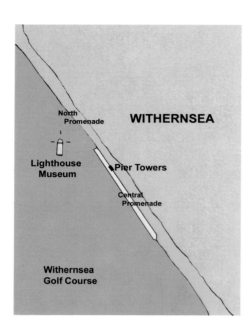

North Promenade

WITHERNSEA

Lighthouse Museum

Pier Towers

Central Promenade

Withernsea Golf Course

Withernsea

coastal defences began in the 1930s. Thankfully the iconic towers were retained and refurbished and provide an eye catching tribute to the past.

Another striking feature of Withernsea is the unusual inland lighthouse which stands in the middle of the town. It is open to the public and stands 127 feet high. If you have the energy to climb the 144 steps you will be well rewarded by superb all round views from the lamp room. It also houses two small museums, one dedicated to the R.N.L.I. and the other to the late actress Kay Kendall. The Withernsea lifeboats and crews saved 87 lives between 1862 and 1913. The lighthouse was decommissioned in 1976. Kay Kendall was born in Withernsea and her grandfather helped build the lighthouse in 1892. He was the last coxswain of the deepsea lighthouse. Kay Kendall had an interesting but tragic life. She was born in Hull Road and took her stage name Kendall from her maternal grandmother Marie Kendall, a musical comedy star. She quickly gained a reputation in films both here and America but sadly died from leukaemia at the tender age of just thirty three.

As with other resorts along the east coast, the opening of the railways brought tourists flocking to the town for a cheap and convenient holiday, boosting Withernsea's economy. Mr. Beeching's closure of the railways in 1964 had a huge effect on Withernsea as a pleasure resort with a considerable drop in visitors.

South of Withernsea stretch desolate, flat, windswept dunes leading to Spurn Head. Here reside hundreds of species of rare wildfowl, accompanied by seals. The only permanently manned lifeboat station in Britain is also here. When visiting Withernsea I was impressed by the massive number of wooden piles along the length of the beach and the rocks and concrete blocks piled up along the sea wall. The reason is real cause for concern. The coastline south of Flamborough Head changes dramatically from imposing cliffs to stumpy ledges of crumbling clay. The sea is said to encroach approximately 30 ft. inland each year, hence the need for the piles and blocks to stop erosion and flooding. Let us fervently hope that these measures will allow visitors to enjoy this pleasant little resort for many years to come.

Withernsea is a traditional holiday resort with good beaches which stretch for miles both north and south. It has a recently rebuilt wide promenade on which stand the eye catching Pier Towers. The town is a resort in miniature where most of the facilities are concentrated in an open space near the town centre and provide varied entertainment for holiday makers known locally as 'diggers'. The Pier Towers provide an historic entrance to a pier that was 1200 feet long built in 1877 at a cost of £12,000. Like many such piers it suffered throughout the years by being struck by passing ships. The first impact by a vessel named "The Saffron" took place only three years after the pier was completed. Shortly after the performance was repeated by an unnamed ship, and then further damage was recorded by a Grimsby fishing boat. In 1903 the ship "Henry Parr" smashed into the once grand pier leaving only 50 feet of rubble. This was finally removed when the construction of

R.W. Thornton

Staithes

Index

Bibliography

Whitburn, Then and Now	J. Gordon Holmes	
Seaburn and Roker	Pat O'Brien, Peter Gibson	Chalford
The Changing Face of Seaham, 1928-1992	Tom McNee, David Angus	
Guide to Rural England,	Country Living Magazine	Travel Publishing Ltd.
Northumbria, Kingdom by the Sea	David Bell, Michael W. Marshall	Keepdate Publishing Ltd.
Ports and Harbours of Northumberland	Stafford Linsley	Tempus
Northumberland, Strange but True	Robert Woodhouse	
Northumbria	Robert Colls	The History Press
Land of Tweed	Dawn Macleod	Blackwood
Exploring Northumbria	George Collard	Sutton Publishing Ltd.
Discovering the Borders	Alan Spence	John Donald Ltd.
Sunderland, People and Places	Alan Brett	Black Cat
Whitley Bay 1920	Rudge	
Fishing and Folk	Bill Griffiths	Northumbria University and Press
Hidden Places of Yorkshire	David Gerrard	Travel Publishing Ltd.
A Kingdom by the Sea	Betty James	Hodder and Stroughton

Journey's End

Cobles and coble building suffered harshly some years ago, when the Government, seeking to reduce overfishing of the sea, started paying fishermen to take their boats out of the water. Today very few, if any, cobles are being built. It has become a dying trade. The dearth of cobles, which used to grace our fishing ports, is very noticeable. When we lived in Craster I spent many enjoyable hours out at sea in a coble, helping the local fishermen to haul in their pots of lobster and crab. We would discuss the day's catch over a pint or two in "The Jolly Fisherman"!.

Happy days!